100 WALKS IN
WALES
& THE MARCHES

Produced by AA Publishing
© AA Media Limited 2010

Published by AA Publishing (a trading name of AA Media Limited, whose registered office is Fanum House, Basing View, Basingstoke, Hampshire RG21 4EA; registered number 06112600)

 This product includes mapping data licensed from Ordnance Survey® with the permission of the Controller of Her Majesty's Stationery Office.
© Crown copyright 2010. All rights reserved. Licence number 100021153

ISBN: 978-0-7495-6502-2
A04143

A CIP catalogue record for this book is available from the British Library.
The contents of this book are believed correct at the time of printing. Nevertheless, the publishers cannot be held responsible for any errors or omissions or for changes in the details given in this book or for the consequences of any reliance on the information it provides. We have tried to ensure accuracy, but things do change and we would be grateful if readers would advise us of any inaccuracies they encounter. This does not affect your statutory rights.

We have taken all reasonable steps to ensure that these walks are safe and achievable by walkers with a realistic level of fitness. However, all outdoor activities involve a degree of risk and the publishers accept no responsibility for any injuries caused to readers whilst following these walks. For more advice on using this book see page 11 and walking safely see page 112. The mileage range shown on the front cover is for guidance only – some walks may exceed or be less than these distances.

These routes appear in the AA Local Walks series and *1001 Walks in Britain*.

theAA.com/shop

Printed in China by Leo Paper Group

Picture credits
All images are held in the Automobile Association's own photo library (AA World Travel Library) and were taken by the following photographers:
Front cover C & A Molyneux; 3 D Santillo; 6/7 N Jenkins; 8 I Burgum; 9 D Croucher; 10 S Lewis ARPS.

Opposite: Talybont Reservoir, Brecon Beacons National Park, Powys

Contents

Introduction and Locator Map   8
Using this Book   11

No

Wales
& The Marches

Modern Wales has a buzz, a street credibility born of a new confidence, expressed through art, music and language. But it is still a land of dragons, of druidic landscapes, of mythical warriors, and of poetry.

Wales
& The Marches

The landscape of Wales can compete with the best of anywhere in Britain. There are high jagged mountains in the north and quiet valleys. In the south the Pembrokeshire coastline juts into a foaming sea and the Brecon Beacons soar above wooded vales. To the east are the Marches, a once-troubled land where powerful English overlords once tried to subdue an unwilling populace.

The Industrial Revolution did much to shape the landscape. The southern valleys became a byword for coal mining and iron production. In the north, whole mountainsides kept England in slate roofs. Now these workings have gone and ash and rowan are returning to the valleys, the rare chough is back and the red kite can be seen above the mountain cwms.

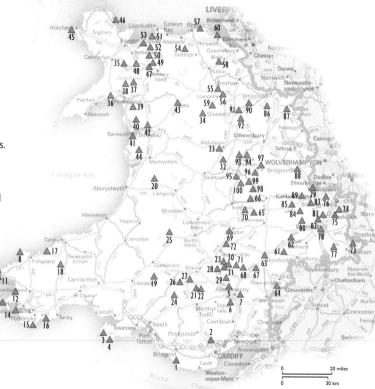

The Black Mountains and the Brecon Beacons

In the east the Black Mountains push up against the English border. Ridges of mountain divide steep valleys – Y Grib offers airy ridge walking, with far-reaching views, west to the Beacons, and east over England. A few outliers around here also make for splendid hill walks. The Blorenge overlooks the World Heritage Site of Blaenavon; the Sugar Loaf commands fine views and its distinctive dome dominates the Abergavenny skyline.

Next are the Brecon Beacons, the high, whalebacked sweeps of sandstone that gave their name to the national park in which they stand. Pen y Fan, is the highest mountain in southern Britain, and also one of the most accessible.

Pembrokeshire Coast

But South Wales also offers the finest coastal walking in Britain, in the Pembrokeshire Coast National Park, which protects a ring of dramatic clifftops from Cardigan to Tenby. Here you can follow the Pembrokeshire Coast Path National Trail for much of the way. At Strumble Head, St David's Head and nearby St Non's Bay you will see majestic

Clwydian Range

The Clwydian Range is also a highlight in the east, and the ascent of Moel Famau from Loggerheads is another classic walk. The short stroll into the Prestatyn Hillside Nature Reserve is where Offa's Dyke, the 182-mile (293km) National Trail begins. At Greenfield near Holywell you'll discover Basingwerk Abbey in a valley which is now a heritage park.

rock scenery and plunging cliffs, as well as remote coves and golden sandy beaches.

Marloes Peninsula and the Angle Peninsula in the mouth of Milford Haven are treats to explore on foot. Highlights include Stackpole, Manorbier and the Gower Peninsula with its sands at Rhossili and Oxwich Bay. Further east is Dunraven Bay, a strip of magnificent Heritage Coast in south Glamorgan.

Moorlands and Valleys

Approaching from the east, the airy moorlands rise up from the English plain. Montgomery and Welshpool make good bases to explore the borderlands. The next valley over carries the River Dee, and walks around Llangollen and Valle Crucis. Further west you will be rewarded with a fine stroll around Bala and Llyn Tegid. Perhaps the best-known uplands in this eastern march are the Berwyns, with one of Wales's loveliest waterfalls, Pistyll Rhaeadr.

Pages 6–7: Mount Snowdon and Llyn-y-Mymbyr, Snowdonia National Park
Above: Rhossili, Swansea
Right: Pistyll Rhaeadr, Powys

Snowdonia

Inevitably you will be drawn along the coast, to Conwy and a lovely stroll on the 'Mountain' above the town. Follow that ridge of hills along and you will encounter some real mountains, the ancient settlement sites and stone circles on Tal y Fan, then beneath the towering massif of the Carneddau at the Bwlch y Ddeufaen, a high mountain pass above the valley of Nant-y-Coed. There are few mountain scenes in Britain that surpass Llyn Idwal, beneath the cliffs of the Twll Du, better known as the Devil's Kitchen. The Llugwy Valley, too, shows the heights of Snowdon to their best effect, viewed from Capel Curig across the twin lakes of Llynnau Mymbyr. You might want to find an easy way up Snowdon, or avoid the crowds and pick off shapely Cnicht. Snowdonia is not all summits: there is a wooded walk around Llyn Crafnant and Llyn Gerionydd.

Anglesey

Ynys Mon, or Anglesey, has a secret mountain on its west coast. At Holyhead you can climb high above the Irish Sea. On the opposite side of the island, Moelfre has its own history of shipwrecks and rescues.

Mid Wales

The Mawddach spills out to the sea at Barmouth, its estuary framed by woodlands and crags. You're in a very Welsh Wales now – no surprise, then, to find Castell y Bere, a great fortress in the Dysynni Valley and Pumlumon, the lonely peak standing above a seldom-visited tract of mid Wales, and yet visible to the hordes in the Brecon Beacons and Snowdonia.

The Borderlands

The River Wye meanders through pastureland as it makes its way south from the cathedral city of Hereford to the Forest of Dean through prime agricultural land. The mighty River Severn is the silver thread which binds together these lush fields, bordered by the whaleback spine of the Malvern Hills to the west and Bredon Hill and the Cotswolds to the east. Here you'll find the cathedral of Worcester and villages where half-timbered houses still survive. Shropshire's hills are dominated by the north-east/south-west ridges of the Stiperstones, the Long Mynd and Wenlock Edge to the east. It is a surprisingly wild part of the Midlands, where heather-covered hills rise from steep-sided valleys.

Bwlch Tyddiad (Roman Steps)
Snowdonia National Park, Gwynedd

Using this Book

❶ Information panels

Information panels show the total distance and total amount of ascent (that is the accumulated height you will ascend throughout the walk). An indication of the gradient you will encounter is shown by the rating 0–3. Zero indicates fairly flat ground and 3 indicates undulating terrain with several very steep slopes.

❷ Minimum time

The minimum time suggested is for approximate guidance only. It assumes reasonably fit walkers and doesn't allow for stops.

❸ Start points

The start of each walk is given as a six-figure grid reference prefixed by two letters indicating which 100km square of the National Grid it refers to. You'll find more information on grid references on most Ordnance Survey maps.

4 Abbreviations

Walk directions use these abbreviations:

L – left
L–H – left-hand
R – right
R–H – right-hand
Names which appear on signposts
are given in brackets, for example
('Bantam Beach').

5 Suggested maps

Details of appropriate maps are given for each walk, and usually refer to 1:25,000 scale Ordnance Survey Explorer maps. We strongly recommend that you always take the appropriate OS map with you. The maps in this book are there to give you the route and do not show all the details or relief that you will need to navigate around the routes provided in this collection. You can purchase Ordnance Survey Explorer maps at all good bookshops.

6 Car parking

Many of the car parks suggested are public, but occasionally you may find you have to park on the roadside or in a lay-by. Please be considerate when you leave your car, ensuring that access roads or gates are not blocked and that other vehicles can pass safely. Remember that pub car parks are private and should not be used unless you are visiting the pub or you have the landlord's permission to park there.

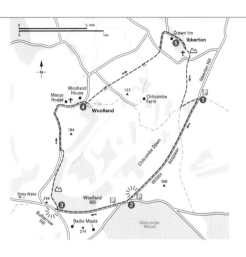

County • REGION

112

LOCATION Walk title
From the tops of Bulbarrow Hill to the valley floor and back, via an atmospheric church.

4.25 miles/6.8km 2hrs **Ascent** 591ft/180m ⚠ **Difficulty** 1
Paths Quiet roads, muddy bridleways, field paths, 2 stiles
Map OS Explorer 117 Cerne Abbas & Bere Regis **Grid ref** ST 791071
Parking Car park at Ibberton Hill picnic site

① Turn **L** along road, following Wessex Ridgeway, with Ibberton laid out below to **R**. Road climbs gradually, and you see masts on Bulbarrow Hill ahead.
② After 1 mile (1.6km) pass car park on **L**, with plaque about Thomas Hardy. At junction bear **R** and immediately **R** again, signposted 'Stoke Wake'. Pass another car park on **R**. Woods of Woolland Hill now fall away steeply on **R**. Pass radio masts to **L** and reach small gate into field on **R**, near end of wood. Before taking it, go extra few steps to road junction ahead for wonderful view of escarpment stretching away west.
③ Go through gate and follow uneven bridleway down. Glimpse spring-fed lake through trees on R. At bottom of field, path swings **L** to gate. Go through, on to road. Turn **R**, continuing downhill. Follow road into Woolland, passing Manor House and Old Schoolhouse, on **L** and **R** respectively.
④ Beyond entrance, on **L**, to Woolland House turn **R** into lane and immediately **L** through kissing

gate. Path immediately forks. Take **L–H** track, down through marshy patches and young sycamores. Posts with yellow footpath waymarkers lead straight across meadow, with gorse-clad Chitcombe Down up **R**. Cross footbridge over stream. Go straight on to cross road. Keeping straight on, go through hedge gap. Bear **L** down field, cross stile and continue down. Cross footbridge and stile to continue along **L** side of next field. Go through gate to road junction. Walk straight up road ahead and follow it **R**, into Ibberton. Bear **R**.
⑤ Continue up this road through village. This steepens and becomes path, bearing **R**. Steps lead up to church. Continue up steep path. Cross road and go straight ahead through gate. Keep straight on along fence, climbing steadily. Cross under power lines, continue in same direction, climbing steadily. Carry on open pasture to small gate in hedge. Do not go through gate, but turn sharp **L**, up slope, to small gate opposite car park.

DUNRAVEN Along The Heritage Coast

A pleasant foray through rolling sand dunes.

6 miles/9.7km 2hrs 30min **Ascent** 460ft/140m ⚠ **Difficulty** ①

Paths Easy-to-follow across farmland and coastline, 5 stiles
Map OS Explorer 151 Cardiff & Bridgend **Grid ref** SS 885731
Parking Large car park at Heritage Centre above Dunraven Beach

❶ Head up lane at back of car park and pass Heritage Centre on **R**. Keep straight ahead as track swings **L** and go through gate to duck into woodland. Continue to fork, and keep **L** to reach stile. Cross and walk along field edge to gate on **L**. Go through gate, then cross stone stile on **R** to keep ahead with hedge **R**.

❷ Cross into another field and keep to **L-H** side, following hedgerow, which is now on **L**. At next stile, continue ahead, pass gate on **L**, to cross another stone stile on **L**. Head **R** over another stile, next to gate, to another stone stile between house and farmyard.

❸ Turn **L** on to road and walk into village. Keep **L** into Southerndown Road then fork **R** into Heol-y-slough. Follow road for 0.75 mile (1.2km) then, as road bends **L**, continue across common. Keep ahead where bridleway crosses track. As you join another track, maintain direction along valley floor.

❹ Path winds down through sand dunes, passing tributary valley on **L**, and eventually emerges on B4524. Cross road and continue towards river until you locate 1 of paths that lead **L**, parallel to river, towards Portobello House. Keep **L** on drive then, once above house, bear **L** to follow clear path through bracken, again parallel to Ogmore River.

❺ Make sure you stay above small cliffs as you approach estuary mouth and to eventually arrive at car parking area above beach. From here, follow obvious track along coast around **L**.

❻ You'll reach dry-stone wall, which funnels through gate marked 'Coast Path'. Continue along coast path until, 1.25 miles (2km) from gate, you meet with very steep-sided valley. Turn **L** into this valley then turn immediately **R**, on to footpath that climbs steeply up grassy hillside.

❼ Stay with footpath as it follows line of dry-stone wall around to West Farm. Keep wall to **L** to continue to upper car park. Wall gap, at back of this, leads you to grassy track that follows road down into Dunraven.

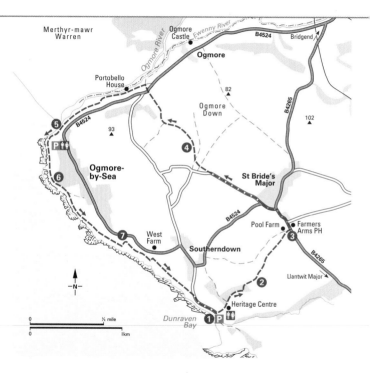

12

CASTELL COCH Fairy-Tale Castle

From a fairy-tale castle to a wild hillside.

5.5 miles/8.8km 2hrs 30min **Ascent** 920ft/280m ⚠ **Difficulty** ②

Paths Forest tracks, disused railway line and clear paths, short section of tarmac, 2 stiles

Map OS Explorer 151 Cardiff & Bridgend **Grid ref** ST 131826

Parking Castell Coch

❶ From car park, walk to castle entrance and turn to **R** to walk to stone information plaque. Take path next to this and climb steeply on good path past waymark post and through fence gap to junction of tracks.

❷ Turn sharp **L**, signposted 'The Taff Trail', by picture of viaduct, and follow this broad track around hillside and then down, where it meets disused railway line close to houses. Pass through barrier on **R** and follow clear track for over a mile (1.6km). Pass picnic area reach barrier.

❸ Go through barrier then, at disused bridge, turn **R** over stile, signposted 'Ridgeway Walk'. Take this and follow it up for few paces and then around to **R**. Ignore1 turn **L** and then turn sharp **L** to zig-zag back across hillside, where you turn **R** again. Follow this around to **L** again, aiming at mast and then, at field edge, bear **R** again. Reach post on narrow ridge; turn **L**.

❹ Climb steeply up ridge and continue, with high ground to **L**, to clear path that leads **L**, to ridge top. Follow this and bear **R** at top to walk easily along, with great views. Keep ahead to drop slightly and then bear **L** on to broad track.

❺ Follow it down through bracken to stile. Cross and take track down to gate that leads on to tarmac drive. Turn **L** and continue past houses on **R-H** side to junction. Turn **R** and climb up to junction; bear **R**.

❻ Carry on past golf club, then fork **R** on to narrow lane that drops and bears **L**. Turn **R** here to walk past Forestry Commission sign and then turn immediately **L**, on to clear footpath marked by post.

❼ Follow path, ignoring tracks **L** and **R**, until posts become blue and reach T-junction by sign forbidding horse-riding. Cross small brook and turn **L** to continue steeply downhill, past turning on **L** to Countryside Visitor Centre.

❽ Track eventually swings around **R** and descends to meet drive. Turn **R** to climb drive and back to castle.

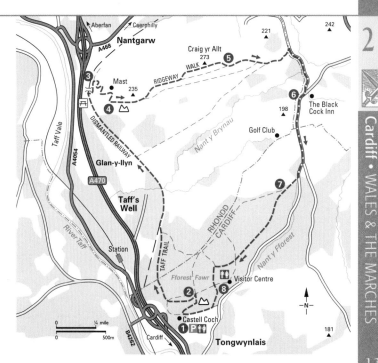

RHOSSILI The High And Lows

This walk takes in the stunning views over one of Wales's finest and wildest beaches.

4 miles/6.4km 1hr 45min **Ascent** 590ft/180m ⚠ **Difficulty** ②

Paths Easy-to-follow footpaths across grassy downs, 2 stiles
Map OS Explorer 164 Gower **Grid ref** SS 416880
Parking Large car park at end of road in Rhossili

❶ From car park, head out on to road and continue uphill as if you were walking back out of village. You'll pass St Mary's Church on your **L** then, immediately after this, bear **L** down on broad track to gate at its end. Go through this and keep **L** to follow grassy track that snakes along steep hillside.

❷ Follow this through bracken, passing Old Rectory on your **L** and eventually you'll reach sunken section with wall on your **L**, and caravan park behind. Don't be tempted to break off **R** just yet; instead, keep going until you come to gate on **L**.

❸ Don't go through but turn sharp **R** and follow grassy track steeply up on to ridge. At top of steep section it's easy to be drawn off to **R** towards some obvious outcrops, but keep to top track that literally follows crest.

❹ You'll pass some ancient cairns and drop slightly to pass a pair of megalithic cromlechs, or burial chambers. These are known as Sweyne's Howes and

are over 4,000 years old. Continue on a broad track up to the high point of The Beacon.

❺ Keep straight ahead on clear track that starts to drop easily then steepens to meet dry-stone wall. Continue walking down side of wall and you'll eventually come to gate you passed through on way out.

❻ Follow lane out to road, turn **R** and pass St Mary's Church on your **R** to return to car park.

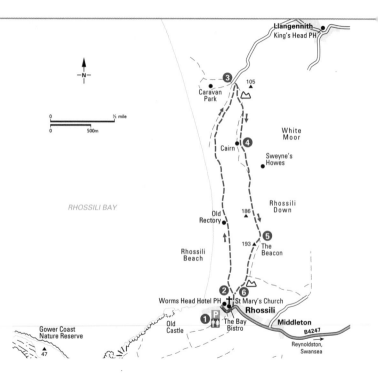

OXWICH Woodland And Coast

An exhilarating ramble through woodland and along delightful coastline.

4.5 miles/7.2km 2hrs **Ascent** 480ft/146m ⚠ **Difficulty** ☐1

Paths Clear paths through woodland, along coast and across farmland, quiet lane, 4 stiles

Map OS Explorer 164 Gower **Grid ref** SS 500864

Parking Oxwich Bay

❶ Walk back out of car park and turn **L** to crossroads. Turn **L** here (waymarked 'Eglwys') and pass Woodside Guesthouse and Oxwich Bay Hotel, on your **R**. This lane leads into woods and up to 6th-century St Illtud's Church, where gate marks end of road and start of path leading out on to Oxwich Point.

❷ Join path that runs beneath church, and follow it for few paces before going up wooden steps that climb steeply into wood. As footpath levels, bear **L** to drop back down through wood and around headland until it comes out into open above Oxwich Point.

❸ Path drops through gorse and bracken to become grassy coast path that runs easily above rocky beach. Keep sea on your **L** and ignore any tracks that run off to **R**. After approximately 1 mile (1.6km) you'll pass distinct valley that drops in from your **R**. Continue past this and you'll be funnelled into narrow, fenced section with field to your **R**. Cross succession of stiles, and

you'll eventually reach path diversion that points you **R**, away from beach.

❹ Follow this to stile and broad farm track, where you turn **L**. Continue up and around to **R** until you come to galvanised kissing gate. Go through this and keep **R** to head up lane past some houses to crossroads.

❺ Turn **R** here and follow road along to fork where you keep **R**. Drop down to entrance of Oxwich Castle on **R**. After looking at or exploring castle, turn **R**, back on to lane, and head down into Oxwich village. Keep straight ahead to car park.

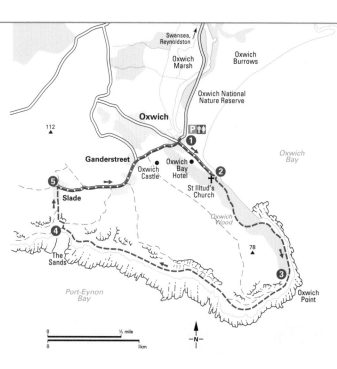

SUGAR LOAF Sweet Walking

Escape the crowds and see another side of one of the most distinctive and popular of the Abergavenny peaks.

4.5 miles/7.2km 2hrs 30min **Ascent** 1,150ft/350m ⚠ **Difficulty** 2
Paths Grassy tracks, no stiles
Map OS Explorer OL13 Brecon Beacons National Park Eastern area **Grid ref** SO 268167
Parking Top of small lane running north from A40, to west of Abergavenny

❶ Standing in car park and looking up slope you'll see 3 obvious tracks leading away. The lowest, down **L**, is tarmac drive; above this, but still heading out **L**, is broad grassy track. Take this and follow it for 500yds (457m) to corner of dry-stone wall.

❷ This marks crossroads where you keep straight ahead, to follow wall on your **L**. Continue along this line for another 0.5 mile (800m), ignoring **R** forks, and keeping wall down to **L**. Eventually, start to drop down into valley, where you leave wall and head diagonally towards wood. At end of wood, keep **L** to descend grassy path to stream.

❸ Climb out of valley, keeping to main, steepest, **R-H** path. This leads around shoulder and meets another dry-stone wall. Follow this, still climbing little, until it levels by corner and gate in wall. Turn **R** here, cross lumpy ground and follow grassy path up.

❹ As track levels, you'll be joined by another track from **L**. Continue ahead and climb on to rocks at western end of summit ridge. Follow ridge to white-painted trig point.

❺ Looking back towards car park, you'll see that hillside is criss-crossed with tracks. Most will lead you back eventually, but easiest route follows path that traverses **R**, from directly below trig point. This veers **L** and drops steeply down blunt spur.

❻ Follow this down until it levels and pass **R** fork and another **R** turn. A track veers **L**, continue past another **R** fork and then take next, to follow almost sunken track along broken wall, which leads to junction by wall. This is track that you followed on outward leg. Bear **L** and retrace steps back to car park.

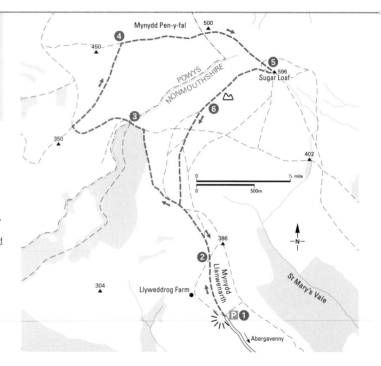

BLORENGE Bird's-Eye View Of Abergavenny

A short sortie and some marvellous views.

3 miles/4.8km 1hr 30min **Ascent** 530ft/161m ⚠ **Difficulty** 1
Paths Clear tracks over open mountainside, quiet lane, no stiles
Map OS Explorer OL13 Brecon Beacons National Park Eastern area **Grid ref** SO 270109
Parking Small car park at Carn-y-gorfydd

❶ From Carn-y-gorfydd Roadside Rest, walk downhill for 500yds (457m) and bear **L**, through green barrier, on to grassy track.

❷ This leads easily uphill, through tangle of bracken, eventually allowing great views over Usk Valley towards outlying peak of Ysgyryd Fawr.

❸ As path levels you'll pass small hut. Continue along escarpment edge, on one of series of terraces that contour above steep escarpment, and enjoy views over Abergavenny and Black Mountains. Rough ground was formed by the quarrying of stone.

❹ Return to hut and bear **R**, on to faint, grassy track that crosses flat ground and small boggy patch before climbing slightly and becoming stony. Away to **R**, you should be able to make out pronounced hump of Bronze Age burial cairn. Path now leads easily to trig point and huge cairn that mark summit.

❺ Continue in same direction, drop down past impressive limestone outcrop and towards huge masts on skyline. You should also be able to see extensive spoil heaps on flanks of Gilwern Hill, directly ahead.

❻ At masts, you'll cross Foxhunter Car Park to meet road where you turn **L** and continue easily downhill, for 600yds (549m), back to start.

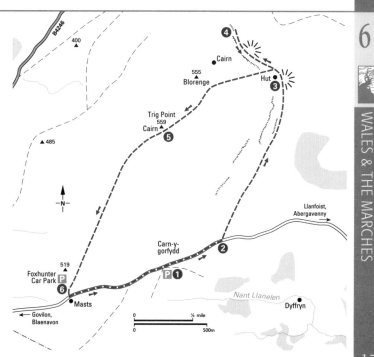

YSGYRYD FAWR Superb Views

A short, steep climb and a skyline walk.

3.75 miles/6km 2hrs **Ascent** 1,150ft/351m **Difficulty** 2

Paths Tracks through woodland and bracken, steep climb and easy traverse of airy ridge, no stiles
Map OS Explorer OL13 Brecon Beacons National Park Eastern area **Grid ref** SO 328164
Parking Small car park at start

❶ Walk through barrier at western end of car park and follow hedged track around to **R**. Climb up to gate and stile beneath large oak tree. Cross these and follow yellow waymarker that directs you off to **R**.

❷ Ascend few wooden steps and keep straight ahead at staggered crossroads, again following yellow marker posts. You'll cross grassy forest track and then climb series of steps to cross another forest track. Continue to gate.

❸ Turn **L** here and follow moss-covered wall around. Wall drops to **L**, but continue along path and shortly you'll come alongside tumbledown wall on **R**. Carry on uphill slightly to cross wall, which drops to **L**, and out on to open ground.

❹ This now undulates as it contours around hillside, eventually leading into narrow rock-strewn valley. Stay on main path to pass small pond on **L** and gradually veer around to **R**. Stay on path and you'll emerge on to open ground with fence to **L**. Continue until your

way ahead is blocked by gate.

❺ Fork **R** in front of gate and follow clear path steeply uphill. Stay on main path, following Beacons Way markers, and eventually you'll reach top of ridge. Turn **R** and follow ridge for few paces to summit.

❻ To descend, retrace steps back to point where you joined ridge and then keep straight ahead to end. Drop down narrow southern spur and bear around to **R** to join stone path. Follow this down to wall and bear **R** to return to gate at Point ❸. Retrace your steps back down through wood to return to car park.

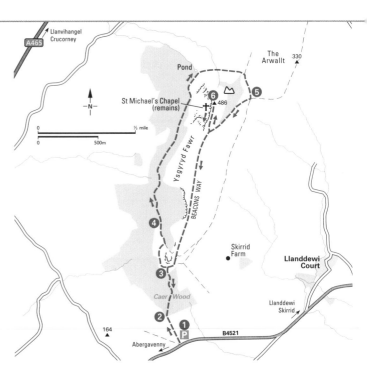

STRUMBLE HEAD An Invigorating Trundle

A walk in the coast's wildest countryside.

8 miles/12.9km 3hrs 30min **Ascent** 920ft/280m ⚠ **Difficulty** ②

Paths Coast path, grassy, sometimes muddy tracks, rocky paths, 13 stiles

Map OS Explorer OL35 North Pembrokeshire **Grid ref** SM 894411

Parking Car park by Strumble Head Lighthouse

❶ Walk back up road and cross gate on **L** on to coast path. Pass above bays of Pwll Bach and Pwlluog, then drop steeply to footbridge behind pebble beach of Porthsychan.

❷ Follow coast path waymarkers around Cnwc Degan and down to bridge, where 2 footpaths lead from coast. Continue along coast, passing cottage on **R** before reaching obelisk at Carregwastad Point.

❸ Follow main path inland and cross stile on to farm track, where you turn **R**, away from coast path. Continue with this path, which is vague in places, up through gorse to wall, then turn **R** on to good track. Take this through gates and around **L-H** bend.

❹ Ignore track to **R** and continue up cattle track, eventually bearing **R** into farmyard where you follow walkway past livestock pens before swinging **L**, after buildings, to road. Turn **R** and follow road past large house to waymarked bridleway on **L**. Pass Trenewydd and go through gate on to green lane. Follow this up

to another gate and on to open ground.

❺ Turn **R** and follow wall to another gate. This leads to walled track which you follow to road. Turn **L** and climb up to car park beneath Garn Fawr. Turn **R**, on to hedged track, and follow this up, through wall gap, and over rocks to trig point.

❻ Climb down and cross saddle between this tor and the slightly lower one to south. From here head west towards even lower outcrop and pass it on **L**. This becomes clear path that leads down to stile. Cross this and turn **L**, then **R** on to drive that leads to road.

❼ Walk straight across and on to coast path. Bear **R** and cross stile to drop down towards Ynys y Ddinas, small island ahead. Navigation is easy following coast path north, over Porth Maenmelyn and up to cairn.

❽ Continue along coast, towards lighthouse, until you drop to footbridge above Carreg Onnen Bay. Cross stile into field, then another back on to coast path and return to car park.

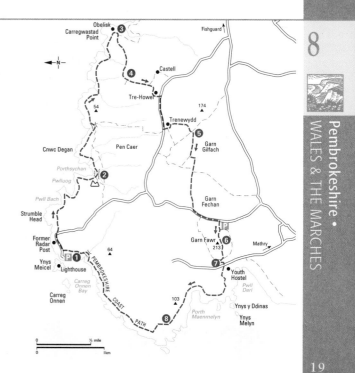

ST DAVID'S HEAD A Rocky Ramble

An easy stroll around dramatic cliffs

3.5 miles/5.7km 2hrs **Ascent** 425ft/130m ⚠ **Difficulty** ☐1

Paths Coast path, clear paths across heathland, 1 stile

Map OS Explorer OL35 North Pembrokeshire **Grid ref** SM 734271

Parking Whitesands Beach

❶ From Whitesands Beach head back up road, pass campsite, and a track on **L**, and then take 2nd track on **L**. Bear **R** where it splits and continue around **L-H** bend to walk up to buildings. Keep **L** to walk between houses, then carry on to gate.

❷ Turn **R** on to open heathland and follow footpath along wall beneath Carn Llidi. Pass track that drops to youth hostel on **R** and continue around to where path splits. Take higher track and continue in same direction until, at corner of wall, clear track runs diagonally **L** towards coast.

❸ Follow this to coast path, where there's large fingerpost, and turn **L** to hug cliff tops. At Porth Llong, path bears **R** to climb to cairn. The headland is labyrinth of paths and tracks, but for maximum enjoyment try to stick as close to cliff tops as possible as you round narrow zawns (clefts). Official coast path doesn't go as far as tip of peninsula, but plenty of other tracks do, so follow one as far as you wish.

❹ From tip, turn **L** and make your way through rocky outcrops on southern side of headland. As you approach Porthmelgan you'll pick up obvious path that traverses steep hillside down into valley, which shelter small stream.

❺ Cross stream and climb up steps on other side. Continue to kissing gate where National Trust land ends and maintain direction. Pass above Porth Lleuog and distinctive rocky promontory of Trwynhwrddyn, worth visiting in its own right.

❻ Path then drops steeply down to road at entrance to Whitesands Beach.

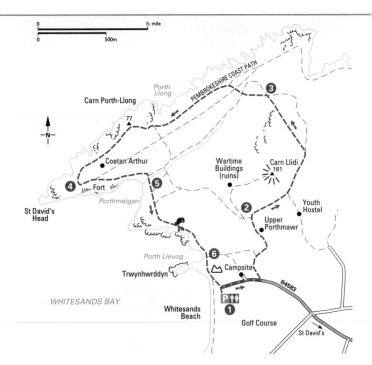

RAMSEY SOUND Pounding The Hermit Monk

Along the shores of Ramsey Sound with great views and plenty of opportunities for spotting wildlife.

3.5 miles/5.7km 2hrs **Ascent** 197ft/60m ⚠ **Difficulty** ☐1

Paths Coast path and easy farmland tracks, 2 stiles

Map OS Explorer OL35 North Pembrokeshire **Grid ref** SM 724252

Parking Car park above lifeboat station at St Justinian's

❶ Walk down to lifeboat station and turn **L** on to coast path, above steps. Follow this, passing above number of lofty, grassy promontories that make great picnic spots. After 0.5 mile (800m), look out for traces of Iron Age earthworks on **L**.

❷ Pass gate and track on **L** – this is your return route – and swing around to west above Ogof Felen. This is a good seal pup beach in autumn. Trail climbs slightly and then drops steeply to ruined copper mine, directly opposite The Bitches.

❸ Continue easily to Pen Dal-Aderyn and then swing eastwards to enter St Brides Bay. Path climbs above some magnificent cliffs and passes between few rocky outcrops before veering north above broad bay of Porth Henllys. Drop down into shallow valley until you come to fingerpost at junction of paths.

❹ Turn **L** to walk away from coast and then cross stile on **R**, into field. Turn **L** to follow track along wall to gate and stile, where you enter courtyard. Keep **L**

here and pass barn to your **L**. When track opens out into field, look for waymark on **R** directing you **R**, through gate on to clear track.

❺ Follow this track down between dry-stone walls to reach another gate, which leads back out on to coast path. Turn **R** and retrace your outward route along grassy clifftop path back to St Justinian's.

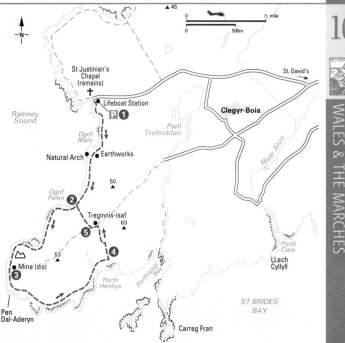

ST NON'S BAY A Pilgrimage

Easy walking around the coastline that gave birth to the Welsh patron saint, St David.

3.5 miles/5.7km 1hr 30min **Ascent** 262ft/80m ⚠ **Difficulty** 1

Paths Coast path and clear footpaths over farmland, 2 stiles

Map OS Explorer OL35 North Pembrokeshire **Grid ref** SM 757252

Parking Pay-and-display car park in St David's

❶ Turn **L** out of car park in St David's and walk down road, as if heading for Caerfai Bay. As houses thin out, you'll see turning on **R** that leads to more dwellings. Take this turning, and then turn **L** on to waymarked bridleway. Follow this bridleway between hedges, past end of road and on to reach junction with another road.

❷ Walk straight across and take waymarked path to fork, where you keep **R** to continue to stile. Cross and keep to **L** of field to another stile, where you keep straight ahead again. This leads to farmyard, which is also caravan park.

❸ Go through gate and turn **L** towards farmyard and then **R**. As drive swings **L**, keep straight ahead with hedge to **R**. Continue across this field and drop down between gorse bushes, keeping straight ahead at crossroads of paths, to road at Porth Clais. Turn **L** to bottom of valley and then, before crossing bridge, turn **L** on to coast path.

❹ Climb steeply on to cliff tops and bear around to **L** to walk towards Porth y Ffynnon. Next small headland is Trwyn Cynddeiriog, where there's a lovely grassy platform above the cliffs if you fancy a rest. Continue walking into St Non's Bay and look for footpath on **L** that leads to ruined chapel.

❺ From chapel, head up to gate that leads to St Non's Well and, from there, follow path beneath new chapel and back out on to coast path. Turn **L** to climb easily on to Pen y Cyfrwy, continue around this and drop down towards Caerfai Bay.

❻ You'll eventually come out beneath Caerfai Bay car park where you turn **L** on to road. Follow this past Diving Centre to St David's and start of walk.

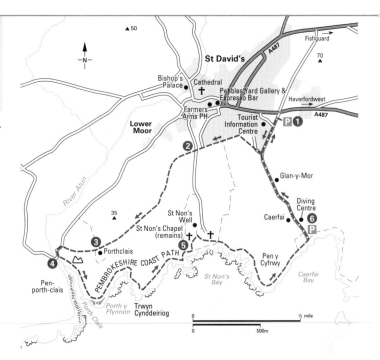

BROAD HAVEN The Haroldston Woods

A winding path through woodland then an easy stroll above the Haroldston cliffs.

3.5 miles/5.7km 1hr 30min **Ascent** 290ft/88m ⚠ **Difficulty** ☐1
Paths Woodland trail, country lanes and coast path, no stiles
Map OS Explorer OL36 South Pembrokeshire **Grid ref** SM 863140
Parking Car park by tourist information centre in Broad Haven

❶ From anywhere in car park, walk towards National Park information centre and follow waymarked path that runs between information centre and coastguard rescue building. Fork **L** at junction with holiday park path and continue to kissing gate, where you cross small footbridge to another junction with path from holiday park. Turn half **R**, through kissing gate, to continue with stream on your **L**.

❷ Cross stream by another bridge and now, with stream and valley floor to **R**, continue easily upwards to T-junction of paths by fingerpost. Turn **R** here, past bench on **R**, and then swing **L** to continue upwards to another junction of paths by small chapel.

❸ Turn **L** to road and then **R** on to it to walk uphill, with church on **R**. Keep ahead at T-junction, then take 1st **L**, towards Druidston Haven. Follow this over cattle-grid to sharp **R-H** bend. Continue for another 300yds (274m) to the Haroldston Chin parking area and gate on **L**.

❹ Go through gate and follow well-surfaced track down towards coast. On reaching cliff tops, bear around to **L** and continue past Black Point.

❺ After passing Harold Stone on **L**, path starts to drop, generally quite easily but there is one steep step. Follow path down to meet road and keep **R** to drop to walkway above beach.

❻ Cross over bridge and then, just before road you are on merges into main road, turn **L** on to tarmac footpath that leads through green and back to car park.

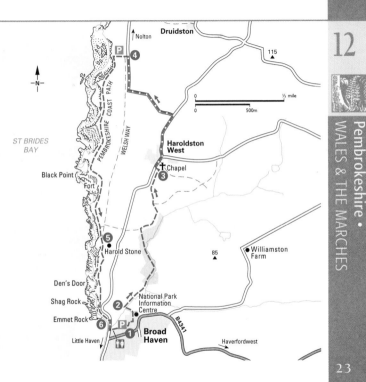

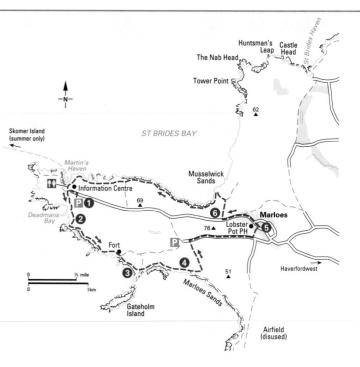

MARLOES Island Views

Around a windswept headland overlooking two islands and a marine nature reserve.

6 miles/9.7km 2hrs 30min **Ascent** 420ft/128m ⚠ **Difficulty** 2

Paths Coast path and clear footpaths, short section on tarmac, 9 stiles

Map OS Explorer OL36 South Pembrokeshire **Grid ref** SM 761089

Parking National Trust car park above Martin's Haven, near Marloes village

❶ From bottom of car park, walk down to bottom of hill. Bear around to **L**, then go through gate straight ahead into Deer Park. Turn **L** and follow path along to gate and out on to coast.

❷ With sea to **R**, continue easily along over Deadman's Bay to stile. The next section cruises along easily, passing earthworks of Iron Age fort on **L** and crossing another stile as you approach Gateholm Island.

❸ It is possible to get across to island at low tide, but care is needed to scramble over slippery rocks. To continue walk, follow coast path, above western end of beautiful Marloes Sands until you drop easily to main beach access path.

❹ Turn **L** and climb up to road; turn **R** here. Follow road along for around 0.75 mile (1.2km) to hedged bridleway on **L**. Follow this down and turn **L** into Marloes village.

❺ Pass Lobster Pot on **L** and continue ahead to leave village. Ignore few tracks on **R**, as road bends around to **L**, and continue out into open countryside where you'll meet footpath on **R**.

❻ Walk down the field edge and bear around to **L** to drop back down on to coast path above Musselwick Sands. Turn **L** and follow path west for over 1.5 miles (2.4km) to Martin's Haven. Meet road and climb past information centre back to car park.

MILFORD HAVEN Its Two Faces

The waters of Milford Haven and the coastline that forms its entrance.

9 miles/14.5km 4hrs **Ascent** 1,017ft/310m ⚠ **Difficulty** [3]

Paths Coast path and easy tracks over agricultural land, short road section, 9 stiles

Map OS Explorer OL36 South Pembrokeshire **Grid ref** SM 854031

Parking Car park at West Angle Bay

❶ Facing sea, walk **L** out of car park and pass between café and the public conveniences to waymarked gate. Follow field edge along, passing through further gates, and eventually leading out on to coast, where **R** fork drops to ruined tower on slender headland.

❷ Continue back up from this, pass through gates and then go down to footbridge. Climb up from this and pass Sheep Island on **R**.

❸ Continue along coast, dropping steeply into succession of valleys and climbing back up each time. At northern end of Freshwater West, keep your eye open for footpath waymarker to **L**.

❹ Cross stile and walk up floor of valley, swinging **L** to stile at top. Cross next field, and another stile, and continue to road (B4320). Turn **L** on to road and walk past houses to **R-H** turn. Follow this to coast and turn **L** on to coast path to merge on to drive.

❺ Take drive to bridleway sign on **R**. If tide is low, you can cross the estuary here and continue along bank of pebbles to road on other side. If it's not, carry on along drive to join road that leads into Angle village and bear **R** by church to follow dirt track over bridge and around to **R**.

❻ Continue around, pass Old Point House Inn on **L** and follow field edges to gravel turning point above lifeboat station on **R**. Keep straight ahead, through gate, and continue through fields into wooded area.

❼ You'll join broad track that runs around Chapel Bay cottages and fort. Keep straight ahead to follow narrow path back above coast. This eventually rounds the headland by Thorn Island.

❽ As you descend into West Angle Bay, path diverts briefly into field to avoid landslide. Continue downwards and bear **R** on to drive that drops you back to car park.

STACKPOLE Beaches And Lakes

An undemanding tour of the clifftops, beaches and lakes at the southernmost point of the Pembrokeshire Coast National Park.

6 miles/9.7km 2hrs 30min **Ascent** 390ft/119m ⚠ **Difficulty** ☐ 1

Paths Easy coast path, quiet lanes and well trodden waterside walkways, no stiles

Map OS Explorer OL36 South Pembrokeshire **Grid ref** SR 976938

Parking National Trust car park above Broad Haven Beach

❶ From car park, head back to National Trust building at head of lane and bear **R**, down set of steps, to beach. Cross beach and keep **L** to walk up creek to footbridge.

❷ Go over this and bear **R** to walk above rocky outcrops, above beach, to gate. Follow grassy path around headland and back inland to gate above Saddle Bay. Continue around large blowhole and up to gate above deeply cloven zawn (cleft), known as Raming Hole.

❸ Go through gate and hug coastline on **R** to walk around Stackpole Head. As you turn back inland, pass blowhole and then go through gate to drop down to Barafundle Bay. Cross back of beach and climb up steps on other side to archway in wall. Continue around to Stackpole Quay.

❹ Turn **L**, above tiny harbour, and drop to pass the Old Boathouse Tearoom on **L** before turning sharp **R**

on to road. Follow this past buildings on **R** and up to T-junction, where you turn **L**.

❺ Drop down into Stackpole village, pass Stackpole Inn on **R**, and continue around series of bends until you come to road on **L**, over bridge.

❻ Cross bridge and bear **L** to follow good path along side of lake. This leads through 1 kissing gate to 2nd where you bear **R**, up short steep section. Continue easily again to bridge.

❼ Don't cross bridge, but drop down on to narrow path that keeps straight ahead and follow it with lake **L**. Continue ahead to another bridge, cross it, then carry on with lake now on **R**. This path leads to footbridge that you crossed at Point ❷. Retrace your steps across beach and up steps back to car park.

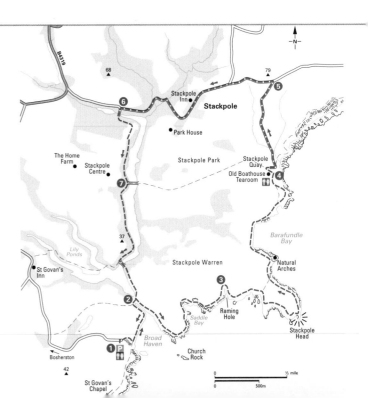

MANORBIER Swanlake Bay

A short stroll across open farmland before taking in a remote cove and some breathtaking coastal scenery.

3 miles/4.8km 1hr 30min **Ascent** 290ft/88m △ **Difficulty** ☐

Paths Coast path, clear paths across farmland, 3 stiles

Map OS Explorer OL36 South Pembrokeshire **Grid ref** SS 063976

Parking Pay-and-display car park by beach below castle

❶ Walk out of car park entrance and turn **L** towards sea. Stay on road as it bears around to **R** and climbs steeply above coast. Pass impressively situated and well-named Atlantic View cottage on **R** before reaching double gate on **L**.

❷ Cross stile and walk along field edge, with bank and fence on **R**, to reach stone step stile. Cross stile and continue heading in same direction to wooden stile close to farm which you also cross. Continue to gate by farmhouse, which brings you into small enclosure, then to wooden stile that leads you away from buildings.

❸ Continue again along field edge to another gate. Go through and turn **L** to drop down field edge to zig-zag that leads on to coast path. Access to beach is more or less directly beneath you.

❹ Turn **L** on to coast path and follow it over another stile and steeply uphill. You'll eventually reach top of

lovely airy ridge that swings east and then north to drop steeply down into narrow dip above Manorbier Bay.

❺ Cross another stile and climb out of dip to continue walking easily above rocky beach. This path leads to drive, beneath large house.

❻ Continue beneath The Dak and uphill slightly to gate, where coast path drops off to **R**. Follow this as it skirts small car park and then winds down through gorse and bracken to beach. Cross stream and turn **L** to follow sandy track back to car park.

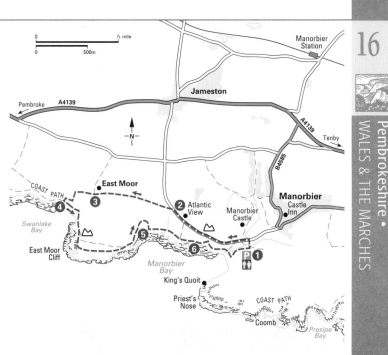

NEWPORT Walk With Angels

Explore Newport then a stiff climb to Carn Ingli, one of Britain's most sacred hilltops.

5.5 miles/8.8km 3hrs 30min **Ascent** 1,080ft/329m ▲ **Difficulty** 2

Paths Easy coastal footpaths, boggy farm tracks, rough paths, 2 stiles
Map OS Explorer OL35 North Pembrokeshire **Grid ref** SN 057392
Parking Free car park opposite information centre, Long Street

❶ Turn **R** out of car park and **L** on to High Street. Fork **L** into Pen y Bont and continue to bridge, where waymarked footpath leads off **L**. Follow this estuary along banks to small road.

❷ Turn **R** on road and walk to its end, where path then follows sea wall. Continue to another lane (signed 'Coast Path'; this is diversion for high tide) and turn **L** to follow it up to A487. Turn **R** on to road, then turn **L** to continue up drive of Hendre farm.

❸ Go through gate, to **L** of buildings, follow track to gate; bear **L** to follow stream. Path emerges on open ground and hugs **L** field edge to gate. Continue in same line along hedged section (boggy). Keep ahead at stile to climb up to road.

❹ Turn **R** on to road and then fork **L** to continue past houses to 2 huge stones on **L**. Pass through stones to follow faint track up to rocky tor. Head up from this towards larger tor of Carn Ffoi. From top of here pick up clearer path through old field system defined by small, ruined walls. Continue to obvious corner of fenced off field.

❺ Bear half **R** on to clear footpath across hillside, aiming towards top of Carn Ingli, which rises ahead of you. Fork **L** after 50yds (46m); continue across hillside beneath high point of Carningli Common. Path bears **R** to climb into saddle between Carningli Common and Mynydd Carningli. Continue to far end of rocky ridge; bear **L** to follow faint path up on to ridge top.

❻ Follow ridge line northwards; drop down, again on faint footpaths, to join clear track straight down hillside. Continue, keeping ahead at 2 crossroads, then turn **L** and then **R** when you get to next junction. This drops you down to gate in corner, which leads on to lane.

❼ Take lane to crossroads and turn **L** to road head, where you turn **R**. Follow this down to junction in College Square, where you turn **L**. Then turn **R**, on to Church Street. Continue into centre and turn **R** into Market Street to main road. Cross into Long Street.

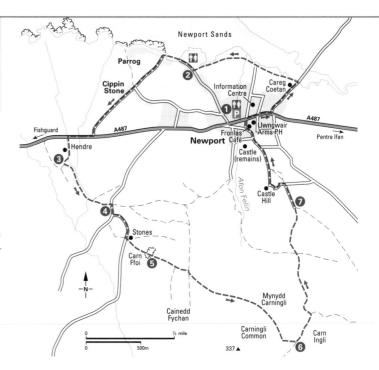

PRESELI HILLS Romancing The Stones
A walk to find some of the planet's most mystical rocks.

5.5 miles/8.8km 2hrs 30min **Ascent** 560ft/170m ⚠ **Difficulty** ☐2
Paths Mainly clear paths across open moorland, no stiles
Map OS Explorer OL35 North Pembrokeshire **Grid ref** SO 165331
Parking Small lay-by on lane beneath Foeldrygarn **NOTE** Navigation very difficult in poor visibility

❶ Walk to **L** out of lay-by on lane from Crymych, then turn **R** up stony track. When you reach gate, keep going ahead for another 100yds (91m) or so, and then fork **L** on to grassy track, which soon becomes clearer as it winds up hillside. Follow this all the way to rocky cairns and trig point on Foeldrygarn.

❷ Bear **L** at summit and locate grassy track that drops steeply south. Cross heather-clad plateau beneath, aiming for **L-H** corner of wood. When you meet main track, turn **R** to walk with edge of wood on **L**.

❸ Leaving wood, path climbs slightly to some rocky tors. 2nd of these, closest to track, has sheepfold at its base. Shortly after this, path forks and you follow **L-H** track down to nearest group of outcrops to **L**.

❹ This is Carn Gyfrwy. Continue on faint paths to larger outcrops ahead, then curve **R** away from stones and drop slightly to Carn Menyn, the lowest, perched precariously on edge of escarpment. Path becomes

clearer here and drops slightly into marshy saddle that can be seen ahead.

❺ In saddle you'll meet main track. Turn **L** and follow it steadily up towards Carn Bica, which is visible on hillside ahead. Just before this, you cross circle made by stones of Beddarthur.

❻ Turn around and retrace steps back to saddle. Climb slightly to pass tor with sheepfold and stay on this main path to walk beside plantation once more, now on **R**. At end of this, drop on grassy track, down to gate. Turn **R** on to lane and continue back to car park.

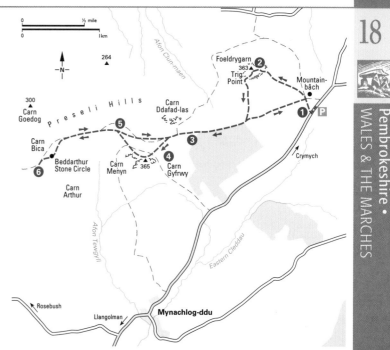

CARMARTHEN FAN The Black Mountain

A walk in spectacular and remote scenery.

7.5 miles/12.1km 4hrs 30min **Ascent** 2,000ft/610m ⚠ **Difficulty** ③

Paths Faint paths, trackless sections over open moorland, no stiles **Map** OS Explorer OL12 Brecon Beacons National Park Western & Central areas **Grid ref** SN 798238 **Parking** End of small unclassified road, southeast of Llanddeusant **NOTE** Best not undertaken in poor visibility

❶ From car park at end of unclassified road, head back towards Llanddeusant and after about 100yds (91m) turn sharp **R**, almost doubling back on yourself, to continue on faint track that contours eastwards around hillside. Follow track as it veers northeast into small valley carved out by Sychnant brook.

❷ Track becomes clear for short period, but don't be drawn uphill to north, instead remain true to course of stream, keeping **L** at confluence with another distinct valley, this one belonging to Nant Melyn.

❸ Track is faint but reasonably easy going up valley, crossing small tributary and following bank above Sychnant. Numerous paths and sheep tracks cross your way, but continue unhindered upwards, aiming for shallow saddle on blunt ridge above. Stream eventually swings to **R** and peters out. At this stage, bear **R** and head along ridge.

❹ You're now aiming for steep and obvious spur of Fan Foel, which lies southeast, approximately 1.5 miles (2.4km) away. Follow whatever tracks you can find over Waun Lwyd and, as ridge starts to narrow, keep to crest where you'll meet path coming up from northeast.

❺ Climb steeply up narrow path on to escarpment and keep **R** to follow escarpment along. Path becomes clearer as it drops steeply into Bwlch Blaen-Twrch. From here, climb up on to Bannau Sir Gaer and continue to summit cairn.

❻ Stay with main footpath and follow edge of escarpment above precipitous cliffs into small saddle or col and up again above Llyn y Fan Fach. Continue around lake, with steep drop to **R**; good path drops down grassy spur to outflow of lake.

❼ Follow this obvious footpath and then, at dam, pick up well-surfaced track that heads back downhill. This leads **R** of waterworks' filter beds and to car park.

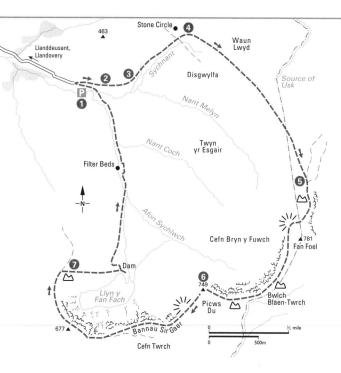

PUMLUMON Remote Lake

Discover a tarn set among the rocks of the Rheidol's dark northern corrie.

5.5 miles/8.8km 3hrs **Ascent** 623ft/190m ⚠ **Difficulty** 1
Paths Good track up, sketchy return path
Map OS Explorer 213 Aberystwyth & Cwm Rheidol **Grid ref** SN 762861
Parking Off-road parking – room for several cars by woods at start of walk, car park by Nant-y-moch dam

❶ From car parking spaces beneath woods east of Nant-y-moch dam (near spot height 392m on OS Explorer maps) walk north along road and take **R-H** fork. Road descends to cross streams of Nant Maesnant-fach and Nant-y-moch before traversing rough moorland along east shores of Nant-y-moch Reservoir. Reservoir, stocked with native brown trout, is popular with anglers during season.

❷ Beneath quarried rocks of Bryn y Beddau, rubble track on **R-H** side of road doubles back up hillside then swings round to **L**. Steep sides of Pumlumon now soar away to skyline on **R**, with little stream of Maesnant tumbling down them. Follow track which climbs further, then levels out to pass shallow lakes, which lie above rocks of Fainc Ddu Uchaf. Now high above bare valleys of Hyddgen and Hengwm track swings south beneath crags of Pumlumon Fach to arrive at Llyn Llygad Rheidol's dam.

❸ To get to footpath along other side you have to ford stream short way downhill – take care if stream is in spate. Path, which runs parallel to eastern banks of stream, is sketchy in places, especially where you ford side stream. It descends peaty terrain where mosses and moor grasses proliferate.

❹ When you reach small stand of conifers in the Hengwm Valley, turn **L** to follow old cart track which fords Afon Rheidol, close to its confluence with Afon Hengwm. Track heads west and soon Hengwm Valley meets that of Afon Hyddgen. Track swings to southwest and passes between squat cliffs of Fainc Ddu Uchaf and western shores of Nant-y-moch Reservoir.

❺ Go through gate above outdoor pursuits centre at Maes Nant and continue along tarmac lane, joining in outward route. Return to car park and start of walk.

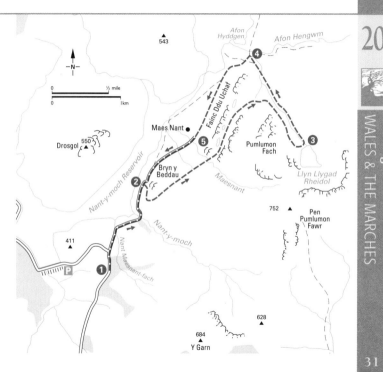

NEUADD RESERVOIRS In The Brecon Beacons

A magical tour of reservoirs, high ridges and mountains.

7.5 miles/12.1km 4hrs **Ascent** 2,395ft/730m ⚠ **Difficulty** ③

Paths Clear well-trodden paths, boggy patches, broad rocky track, no stiles

Map OS Explorer OL12 Brecon Beacons National Park Western & Central areas **Grid ref** SO 032179

Parking At end of small lane leading north from Pontsticill

❶ Continue up lane to small gate, which leads into grounds of reservoir. Bear slightly **L** on to narrow path that drops to cross concrete bridge over outflow. Climb on to bank opposite and bear **L** to walk along its top to gate that leads out on to open moorland.

❷ Go through this and keep straight ahead, taking **L-H** of 2 tracks, which leads easily uphill towards edge of mainly felled forest. Follow clear track up, with forest to **L**, and then climb steeply up stony gully to top of escarpment.

❸ Once there, turn **R** on to obvious path and follow escarpment for over 2.5 miles (4km). Eventually drop into distinct saddle with flat-topped summit of Corn Du directly ahead. Where path forks, keep ahead and climb easily up on to summit. Follow escarpment edge along and then drop into another saddle; now take path up on to next peak, Pen y Fan.

❹ Again, from summit cairn, follow escarpment around and drop steeply, on rocky path, down into

deep col beneath Cribyn. Keep ahead to climb steeply up to cairn on narrow summit. Note: this climb can be avoided by forking **R** and following another clear path that contours **R** around southern flanks of mountain and brings you out at Point 6.

❺ From top, bear slightly **R** and follow escarpment around to southeast. After long flat stretch, drop steeply into deep col (Bwlch Ar y Fan).

❻ Turn **R** on to well-made track that leads easily down mountain. Go through gate and follow track for over 1.5 miles (2.4km), until it starts to swing slightly **L** and drops steeply into rocky ravine. Turn **R** here on to track and take it down to gate. Go through this, turn **L** and follow track to its end. Turn **R** in front of gate on to another track that leads back to gate at head of lane. Go through gate and follow lane back to start.

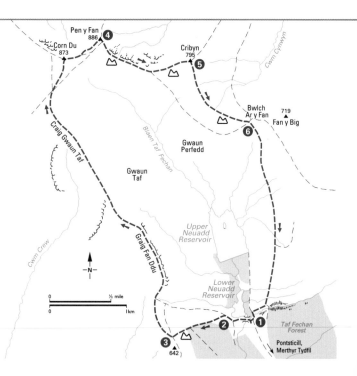

CAERFANELL VALLEY Skyline Walking

Spectacular escarpments above a wild and remote valley.

5.5 miles/8.8km 3hrs 30min **Ascent** 1,542ft/470m ⚠ **Difficulty** ☐2

Paths Clear tracks across open mountain tops, along river and through forest, some mud and wet peat, 3 stiles **Map** OS Explorer OL12 Brecon Beacons National Park Western & Central areas
Grid ref SO 056175 **Parking** Large car park at start, 3 miles/4.8km west of Talybont Reservoir

❶ Walk back out of car park, either crossing cattle grid or stile to **L** of it, then turn immediately **R** on to stone track that heads uphill, with stream **L**. Follow this track steeply up to top of escarpment and keep straight ahead to cross narrow spur, where you bear around, slightly to **L**, to follow escarpment.

❷ Stay on clear path, with escarpment to **R**, for about 1.5 miles (2.4km), till you meet paths at head of valley.

❸ Take sharp **R** turn to follow narrow track slightly downwards, around head of valley, towards cliffs that can be seen on opposite hillside. Keep **L** at fork and continue to crash memorial.

❹ Almost directly above memorial, rocky gully leads up on ridge. On **L-H** side of this, as you look at it, is faint track that climbs steeply up. Take this to top and turn **R** on to narrow but clear track. Follow this track easily above crag, to distinctive cairn at southern end of ridge. Just north of cairn is small stream.

❺ Follow this down for 10ft (3m) to join clear grassy track that trends **L** at first, then follows clear groove down spur. This becomes easy footpath that crosses broad plateau and then leads to junction at wall. Turn **R** here and drop down to Afon Caerfanell.

❻ Cross stile on **L** at bottom and follow narrow footpath downstream, past waterfalls. Eventually pass largest of them and come to footbridge.

❼ Cross footbridge and then stile to follow track into forest. Pass some ruined buildings on **R**; before crossing small bridge, turn **R** on to clear path that leads uphill into forest with waterfalls **L**.

❽ Continue uphill on main track, taking optional detours to **L** and **R** to see other waterfalls. Eventually meet broader forest track; turn **L** then **R** to return to car park.

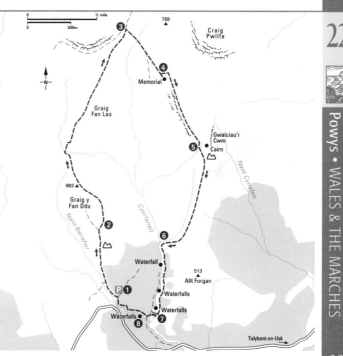

WAUN FACH From The Grwyne Fawr Valley
The easiest way on to the Black Mountain.

9.25 miles/14.9km 4hrs **Ascent** 2,000ft/610m ⚠ **Difficulty** 3

Paths Clear tracks over open moorland, one indistinct path over boggy ground, steep descent, 1 stile
Map OS Explorer OL13 Brecon Beacons National Park Eastern area **Grid ref** SO 252284
Parking Car park at head of lane at start **NOTE** Difficult navigation in poor visibility

❶ Take broad track at far end of car park and follow it out on to road. Turn **R** to continue up valley then, after about 300yds (274m), fork **R** on to stony track along bottom of forest. Follow this track and continue through 2 gates to 3rd gate, by stand of trees, above Grwyne Fawr Reservoir.

❷ Keeping trees to **L**, carry on past reservoir and up valley. Go through another gate and continue until track finally fords Grwyne Fawr stream. Stay on stony track, which now peters out to become grassy before deepening into obvious rut. Continue on to flat ground above steep northern escarpment, where path meets fence by stile on **R**.

❸ Turn **L** on to clear track and then, after 100yds (91m), turn **L** again on to faint grassy track up front of blunt spur. Follow track over numerous peaty hollows to summit plateau of Waun Fach, identified by large concrete block.

❹ Continue in same direction (southeast) across large expanse of boggy ground. There's no clear path on this section, but there are usually plenty of footprints in wet ground leading towards obvious cairn topped peak of Pen y Gadair Fawr, at far end of ridge. In saddle between 2 summits, pick up faint path that follows eroded line of stream.

❺ Path improves as it continues, eventually leaving stream behind and making beeline for peak ahead. Climb to cairn, then continue in same direction to drop steeply for 10yds (9m). As it levels, path splits. Fork **L** on to faint grassy track that drops slightly and then turns **R**, to edge of forest.

❻ Turn **L** to head down steep hillside, with forest R. Follow this path down to river at bottom where you turn **R**, over stile. Continue along riverbank for about 400yds (366m), then cross bridge to road. Turn **R** on to this to return to car park.

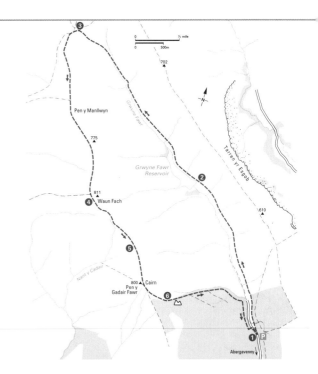

PORTH YR OGOF Along The Waterfalls

Riverside scenery and four waterfalls.

4 miles/6.4km 2hrs **Ascent** 360ft/110m ⚠ **Difficulty** ☐2

Paths Riverside paths and forest tracks, some rough sections and steps, no stiles
Map OS Explorer OL12 Brecon Beacons National Park Western & Central areas **Grid ref** SN 928124
Parking Park car park at Porth yr Ogof, near Ystradfellte

❶ Cross road at entrance to car park and head down **L-H** of 2 paths, waymarked with yellow arrow. Ignore **R** fork marked 'Cavers Only' and follow main path through kissing gate and on to river bank. Now keep river to **R** to follow rough footpath through 2 more kissing gates to reach footbridge.

❷ Don't cross but continue ahead, to climb steeply up to fence. Stay with path, with wooden fence now on **R**, for few paces to junction of footpaths marked with large fingerpost. Bear sharp **L** on to well-surfaced track, waymarked to Gwaun Hepste, and follow this for short distance to another junction, where you should turn **R** (waymarked 'Sgwd yr Eira').

❸ Continue walking along well waymarked forest trail until another fingerpost directs you **R**, downhill. Follow this track to edge of forest and then bear around to **R**. This track leads to top of wooden steps, on **L**.

❹ Go down steps to Sgwd yr Eira (Waterfall of the Snow) and then, having edged along bank and walked behind falls (waterproofs recommended), retrace steps up to edge of wood. Turn **L** and continue, still following red-banded posts, to fork marked with another fingerpost.

❺ Turn **L** here (waymarked to Sgwd Isaf Clun-gwyn) and descend to riverside. Turn **L** again to Sgwd y Pannwr (Fullers Falls), then turn around to walk upstream to Sgwd Clun-gwyn Isaf (Lower Waterfall of the White Meadow). Take care, ground is very steep and rough around best viewpoint.

❻ Retrace your steps downstream to original descent path and turn **L** to climb back up to fork at top. Turn **L** and follow red-banded waymarkers along to Sgwd Clun-gwyn Isaf, where there's fenced viewing area. From here, continue along main trail to place where you split off earlier.

❼ Drop back down to footbridge and continue along riverbank to Porth yr Ogof.

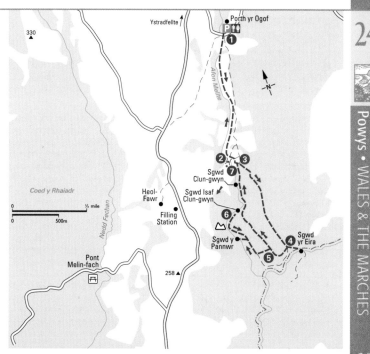

CWM GWESYN Walk On The Wild Side

9.5 miles/15.3km 6hrs **Ascent** 2,000ft/610m ⚠ **Difficulty** 3

Paths Riverside path, faint or non-existent paths over moorland, some good tracks, some awkward stream crossings, no stiles **Map** OS Explorer 200 Llandrindod Wells & Elan Valley **Grid ref** SN 860530
Parking Car park northeast of Abergwesyn **NOTE** Difficult navigation, avoid in poor visibility

❶ Turn **R** on to road to bridge, take track up **L**. Turn **R**, through gate. Follow track to Afon Gwesyn; ford it. Reach gate and go up towards wood where track splits. Choose top option and then, as this bends **L** and heads downhill, fork **R**, to traverse clearing to gap in wood.

❷ Follow path down to ford. Climb to open ground; bear **R** to farm track by buildings. Turn **L**; go through gate; fork **L** under crags; continue to open ground. Follow east side of valley 1.5 miles (2.4km) to waterfall.

❸ Pass it on **R**, then continue until path almost disappears. Follow stream to distinctive small ridge coming in from **R**. Take this for 100yds (91m); bear **L** on narrow path around boggy patches until summit of Drygarn Fawr becomes visible.

❹ Climb slope to trig point; follow ridge east past 2 cairns. You'll see 2 summits, 1.5 miles (2.4km) away; one with cairn on top is Carnau, your next objective. Track descends east from cairn. Follow this until it levels and rounds **L-H** bend, faint path forks **R** at start of careful navigation; if you're in any doubt about visibility,

retrace your tracks.

❺ Follow track, which links boundary stones for 200yds (183m), until you see 1 stone offset **R** of path. Turn sharp **R** here (south), away from path, and cross wet ground to climb slightly on broad rounded ridge. Head of valley is ahead. As you drop into this, bear slightly **L** to follow high ground (valley **R**). Continue on sheep tracks to cross 2 hollows, to grassy hilltop. See cairn ahead. Take clear path that leads to it.

❻ From Carnau you'll see start of gorge to southwest. Walk towards it, and pick up good track across river. Continue downstream on far bank; stay with path as it bears **R** and crosses open hillsides before dropping into valley bottom. Ford stream to go through gate.

❼ Climb on track across stream; continue to 5-way junction. Turn sharp **R**, enter gate and 2nd gate **L**. Drop through field on track. Follow it to junction above houses on **L**. Keep **R**, cross stream; take track across field to path junction. Keep ahead, descend through Glangwesyn yard to road. Turn **R** to return to your car.

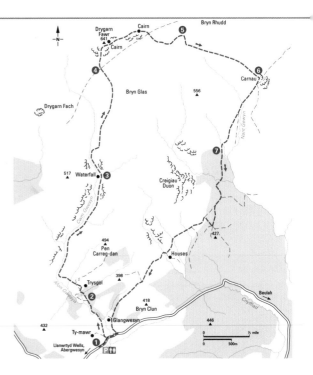

CRAIG CERRIG-GLEISIAD Back To Nature

The formidable crags of one of the Beacon's best-known nature reserves.

4 miles/6.4km 2hrs **Ascent** 1,050ft/320m ⚠ **Difficulty** 2
Paths Clear footpaths and broad stony tracks, 2 stiles
Map OS Explorer OL12 Brecon Beacons National Park Western & Central areas **Grid ref** SN 972221
Parking Pull-in by small picnic area on A470, 2 miles (3.2km) north of Storey Arms

❶ There's bridge and small picnic area at southern end of lay-by. Walk towards this and go through adjacent kissing gate (signposted to Twyn Dylluan-ddu and Forest Lodge). Head towards crags, following clear footpath, until you come to gap in next wall.

❷ Pass through this and turn **R** to follow dry-stone wall north. Head down into small valley, cross stream, then stile to continue in same direction. Drop into another, steeper, valley and climb out, still following track. Continue through bracken to stile.

❸ Cross and turn **L** on to stony track. Follow this up to gate and stile and continue through rough ground, churned up by mining, until it levels on dished plateau. Bear **R** here to whitewashed trig point of Fan Frynych, then turn sharp **L** to return to main track above escarpment.

❹ Turn **R** on to main track again and continue past more rough ground before dropping slightly into broad but shallow valley. Near bottom, go over stile on **L** (signed 'Beacons Way').

❺ Follow obvious path straight ahead and cross top of steep hillside to cairn. Turn **R** here to drop steeply all way down into heart of nature reserve, following regular waymark posts.

❻ As ground levels, bear around **R** to follow signed diversion and continue alongside stream to gap in wall you passed through earlier. Go through again and follow outward path back to car park.

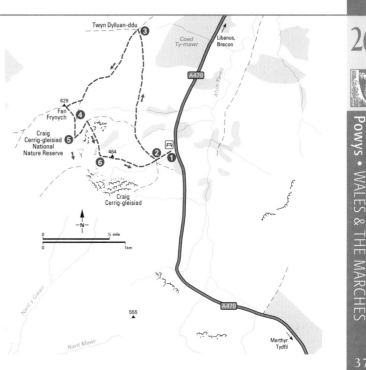

PEN Y FAN The Beacons Horseshoe

The connoisseur's way up to the high ground.

7 miles/11.3km 4hrs **Ascent** 2,100ft/640m ⚠ **Difficulty** ③

Paths Well-defined paths and tracks, short distance on quiet lanes, 5 stiles

Map OS Explorer OL12 Brecon Beacons National Park Western & Central areas **Grid ref** SO 025248

Parking Car park at end of small lane, 3 miles (4.8km) south of Brecon

❶ Walk uphill from car park and pass information plinth before crossing stile. Walk along **R-H** side of field towards top **R-H** corner and then bear **L** to continue along fence to another stile.

❷ Follow broad but faint grassy track straight on. As it reaches steeper ground, it becomes better-defined stony track that swings slightly **L** and climbs hillside. Continue ahead, up towards head of Cwm Gwdi, and keep ahead, ignoring **R** forks, until path eventually levels out on Cefn Cwm Llwch.

❸ Continue along ridge towards summit ahead. At foot of peak, track steepens considerably, offering a fine. Continue to climb steeply over rocky steps to summit cairn on Pen y Fan.

❹ Bear **R** to follow escarpment edge along and drop into shallow saddle beneath rising crest of Corn Du. Continue up on to this summit, then bear **L** for few paces to locate steep path that drops down through

rocky outcrops on to easier ground below. Bear **R** and drop past summit.

❺ Continue downhill and pass Tommy Jones obelisk with steep crags of Craig Cwm Llwch on **R-H** side. Above lake, path forks; take **R-H** option and drop steeply, around dog-leg and over moraine banks to lakeshore.

❻ Clear track leads north from lake – alongside outflow; follow it over easy ground to cross stile on to broad farm track. Take this down to gate in front of building and climb stile on **L**. Cross compound and climb another stile to follow waymarker posts around to **R** on to another track, beyond building.

❼ Bear **L** on to this track and follow it down, over footbridge, to parking area. Keep ahead, through gate to T-junction, where you turn **R**. Cross bridge and continue for over 1 mile (1.6km) to another T-junction. Turn **R** and walk uphill back to car park.

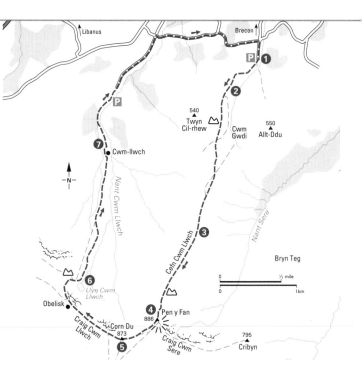

Y GRIB An Airy Stroll

A strenuous climb on to the Black Mountains via one of the Beacon's finest ridges.

8 miles/12.9km 4hrs 30min **Ascent** 1,960ft/597m ▲ **Difficulty** ③
Paths Clear tracks over farmland, rolling moorland and narrow ridge, quiet lane, 3 stiles
Map OS Explorer OL13 Brecon Beacons National Park Eastern area **Grid ref** SO 175295
Parking Castle Inn, Pengenffordd, allows parking for small fee

❶ Wooden steps go down from back of car park on eastern side of road. These lead on to rough track; turn **R** and then immediately **L** over stile. Follow permissive path down side of wood to stream, cross it and clamber over another stile.

❷ Keep to **L** field edge (wood on **L**) and climb to the top of field. Leave wood and follow fence line upwards to another stile. This leads on to flanks of Castell Dinas.

❸ Keep ahead here to cross ruins and descend steeply into deep saddle. Cross broad track, then climb directly up steep spur ahead. You're now on Y Grib and it's possible to follow faint track to cairn and then down to small notch where route is crossed by bridleway.

❹ Climb steeply back out of this and hug crest up to another cairn. Now keep ahead on fainter path that passes another cairn before climbing steeply, straight ahead, on to broad spur of Pen y Manllwyn.

❺ Here, at small cairn, turn **R** on to clear track that over top of Pen y Manllwyn and up to boggy plateau on top of Waun Fach. Summit is marked by concrete block that used to act as trig point base. Turn **R** and follow obvious path down on to ever-narrowing spur of Pen Trumau.

❻ Cross narrow summit and, as ground steepens, follow path through rocky outcrops to broad saddle, marked by large cairn. Turn sharp **R** here and follow main track as it descends, easily at first. This steepens and becomes rocky for before it reaches gate above walled track.

❼ Follow track down to road and turn **R**, then immediately **L**. Drop to bottom of valley and climb out again on other side. As road turns sharply to **L**, bear **R** on to stony farm track that runs between hedgerows. Follow track past stile you crossed earlier, on **R-H** side, then take steps on **L**, back to car park.

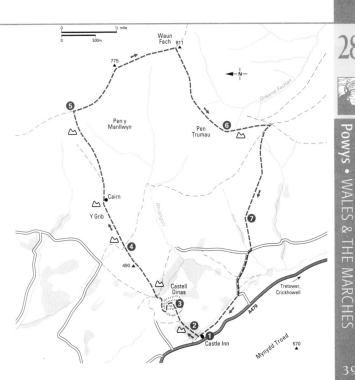

PEN CERRIG-CALCH The Crickhowell Skyline

Views of Crickhowell and the remote valleys of the central Black Mountains.

8.5 miles/13.7km 4hrs 30min **Ascent** 1,700ft/518m ⚠ **Difficulty** 3

Paths Waymarked footpaths, clear tracks, 7 stiles
Map OS Explorer OL13 Brecon Beacons National Park Eastern area **Grid ref** SO 234228
Parking Car park beneath small crag and next to bridge, in narrow lane running north from Crickhowell

❶ Walk back over bridge and bear **R** up ramp that leads to 2nd gate on **R**. Cross stile to **R** of gate and walk up field edge to another stile that leads on to lane. Cross this and climb over another stile to continue, with wood on **L**, up to yet another stile in dry-stone wall.

❷ Cross this and turn **L** to follow faint path around hillside through bracken. Walk alongside wall to clear offset crossroads, where wall drops away, keep straight ahead here and rejoin wall shortly. Continue straight across another section where wall drops away and then joins path again.

❸ Next time it drops, keep straight ahead again to meet it at pronounced corner, marked with post. Turn **R** on to clear track that leads straight up on to summit of Table Mountain.

❹ Turn off plateau at its narrowest northern point and cross saddle on obvious track. This climbs steeply up on Pen Cerrig-calch. As path levels, ignore track to

L and keep straight ahead to trig point.

❺ Continue ahead to drop slightly down small crag to meet escarpment edge. Continue along ridge, which narrows slightly, then climb again to narrow summit of Pen Allt-mawr.

❻ Path leads down steep northern spur. Take path starts to climb, reach parting of paths.

❼ Fork **R** and continue to small cairn on narrow ridge top that leads southwest. Follow ridge easily down to cross quarried ground and reach large cairn. Keep ahead to walk down to stile at top of plantation. Cross this and keep ahead again to follow rutted track alongside plantation down to another stile.

❽ This leads to sunken track; follow it down to path junction. Keep ahead, through gate, and head along field top to marker post that sends you **L**, downhill. Bear **L** at bottom to stile by gate to car park.

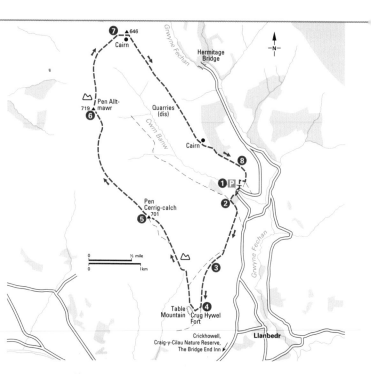

CAPEL-Y-FFIN Llanthony And Its Hills

A demanding trek.

9.5 miles/15.3km 5hrs 30min **Ascent** 2,460ft/750m ⚠ **Difficulty** ③
Paths Easy-to-follow paths, steep slopes, open moorland, muddy lowland trails, 10 stiles
Map OS Explorer OL13 Brecon Beacons National Park Eastern area **Grid ref** SO 255314
Parking Narrow pull-in at southern edge of Capel-y-ffin, close to bridge

❶ Walk towards bridge. Don't cross, but bear **L** up lane ('The Grange Pony Trekking Centre'). Follow this past footpath on **L**. Continue to drive **L** to trekking centre, and follow this up to barns.

❷ Keep **R** and on to house on **R** with gate. Bear **L**; climb to another gate. Go through and follow eroded to easier ground. Cross source of small stream, and continue to foot of steep zig-zag track up escarpment.

❸ Follow this then, as gradient eases, continue on broad and often boggy track. Take this past small cairns to large Blacksmith's Anvil at ridge top. Turn **L** and follow track south over Chwarel y Fan.

❹ Continue along ridge to summit of Bal-Mawr. Go down to **L** and pass good track on **L-H** side. Keep ahead to cairn and descend **L**. Drop to fork; keep **R** to follow brook to crossroads. Maintain direction (signposted 'Cwm Bwchel').

❺ Continue through 2 fields, past house, and over stile. Ignore stile on **R** and continue down to stile at field bottom. Cross, bear **R**; cross stile and footbridge. Keep ahead to next stile and on to gate. Follow stream to footbridge. Cross and take lane to road. Turn **L**, then **R** to visit priory.

❻ Enter gate **L**, in front of priory (' Hatterrall Hill'), and follow track to stream; turn **L** to gate. Continue through fields and small copse to interpretation board. Follow path on to ridge and to crossroads; turn **L** at Offa's Dyke.

❼ Walk along dyke, pass trig point and continue for 1 mile (1.6km) to cairn and marker stone at crossroads of paths. Turn **L**; follow path around **L-R** zig-zag to wall. Turn **R** then **L** over stile. Walk down, over hedge stile next field bottom. Turn **R** to stile on **L** on to lane. Turn **R** and follow through yard, where it becomes rough track. Keep ahead to sharp **L-H** bend and keep ahead, up steps and over stile. Continue ahead through fields to join lane and follow this past 2 chapels to road. Turn **L** to car.

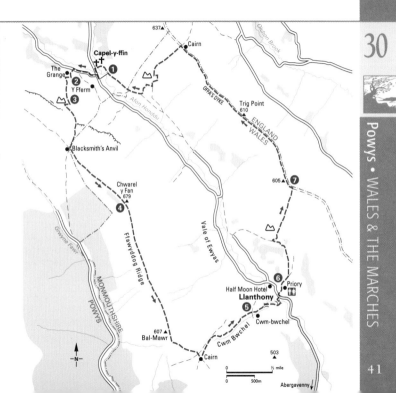

CAPEL-Y-FFIN Tackling The Vale of Ewyas

A variation of the previous walk as you trek around the head of the Ewyas Valley.

9 miles/14.5km 4hrs **Ascent** 1,560ft/475m ⚠ **Difficulty** 2

Paths Easy-to-follow tracks, steep slopes, open moorland, 2 stiles

Map OS Explorer OL13 Brecon Beacons National Park Eastern area **Grid ref** SO 255314

Parking Narrow pull-in at southern edge of village, close to bridge

❶ Walk towards bridge, but before you cross it, bear **L** up lane ('The Grange Pony Trekking Centre'). Follow this alongside of stream and past footpath on **L**, marked by stone archway. Continue to drive on **L**, again leading to trekking centre, and follow this up to barns.

❷ Keep **R**; continue uphill to large house on **R**, with gate blocking progress ahead. Bear around to **L** and climb on loose track to another gate. Enter and follow a rough, eroded track zig-zagging up to easier ground. Cross source of small stream, and continue to foot of steep zig-zag track up escarpment.

❸ Follow this then, as gradient eases, continue ahead on broad, often boggy, track. Take this past small cairns to large atop ridge. Turn **R** and follow track easily over Twyn Talycefn to trig point on Pen Rhos Dirion. (Summit can be avoided by clear path that traverses **L** before final climb.) Turn **R** and drop steeply through heather into broad saddle.

❹ Keep ahead over flat section; climb steeply up on to Twmpa. Turn **R**; bear **L** on to track that follows line of east-facing escarpment. Continue until ridge narrows and drops steeply away.

❺ Descend directly to large square cairn; keep ahead down steep spur and as it becomes too steep, zig-zag **L-R**, to cut steep line through bracken to junction with broad contouring bridleway. Keep ahead to cross this and drop down to join stony track alongside wood.

❻ Turn **L** to follow this down to gate and keep ahead between 2 houses. At drive, keep ahead to cross stile and continue in the same direction over stile in bottom corner. Turn **R** to follow lane to car.

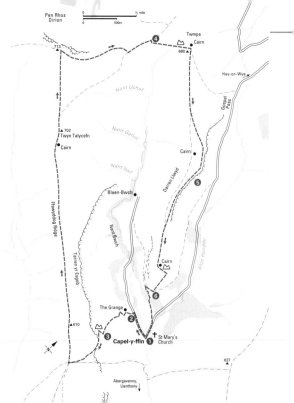

MONTGOMERY Marcher Lords Land

Iron Age and medieval castles and views across a wide landscape.

5.25 miles/8.4km 3hrs **Ascent** 951ft/290m ⚠ **Difficulty** 2
Paths Well-defined paths, farm tracks and country lanes, 1 stile
Map OS Explorer 216 Welshpool & Montgomery **Grid ref** SO 224963
Parking Car park on Bishops Castle Street on B4385 at south end of town

❶ From car park head north, then **L** along Broad Street, where you'll see town hall and The Dragon Hotel. Signpost to castle points up lane behind, path then leaving **R** through kissing gate. It's a must to see and is free. Return to this point. Head north up Arthur Street, past Old Bell Museum.

❷ Reaching main road, go **L** and keep **L** with B4385 in direction of Newtown. Leave just past speed de-restriction sign, over stile on **L**. Bear **R** across field towards trees. This path climbs through woodland, then swings **L** (southwest) to reach old hilltop fort above Ffridd Faldwyn.

❸ Over stile at far side of fort, bear **L** downfield to roadside gate. Turn **L** along road, which takes you back towards Montgomery.

❹ As road turns sharp **R** just above town, leave it for footpath on **R** signposted for Montgomeryshire War Memorial and beginning beyond kissing gate. Footpath climbs steadily uphill to join farm track, which at first runs parallel to Town Ditch.

❺ As it enters high pastures, track begins to level and traverse eastern hillside. Here you can make a detour to the war memorial that can be seen clearly ahead at the top of the hill. Return to track and follow it through gate and past pens with gorse and hawthorn lining way on **L**.

❻ Keep going in next field, hedge curving into corner. Walk ahead through wide gap and head downfield to leave by gate and stile at bottom. Follow tarmac track down to junction southeast of Little Mount farm and go **L** to lane.

❼ Keeping **L** at successive junctions, walk back to Montgomery. Turn **R** along Kerry Street into square.

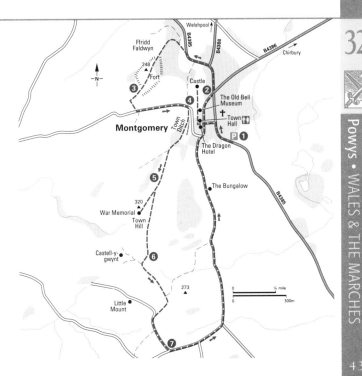

33

POWIS CASTLE The Montgomery Canal

See how the Earls of Powis lived as you walk through their deer park and past their huge red palace on the hill.

4 miles/6.4km 2hrs **Ascent** 328ft/100m ⚠ **Difficulty** 1
Paths Tarmac drive, field path, canal towpath, 3 stiles **Map** OS Explorer 216 Welshpool & Montgomery
Grid ref SJ 226075 **Parking** Large pay car park off Church Street, Welshpool

❶ From main car park go past tourist information centre then **L** along Church Street. At crossroads in town centre turn **R** to head up Broad Street, which later becomes High Street.

❷ When you get just beyond town hall, turn **L** past small car parking area and pass through impressive gates of Powis Castle Estate. Now follow tarmac drive through park grounds and past Llyn Du (Black Lake).

❸ Take **R** fork, high road, which leads to north side of castle. Detour from walk here to visit the world-famous gardens and the castle with its fine paintings and furniture and works of Indian art collected by Robert Clive. Continue on walk on high road and follow it past 2 pools on **L** and Ladies Pool on **R** to reach country lane.

❹ Turn **L** along country lane. Opposite next estate entrance leave lane over stile beside gate on **R**, from which grass track winds down to bridge. Climb away

beside R-H fence. Continue over another stile in corner along old way, which gently falls to lane beside Montgomery Canal. The canal, which runs for 33 miles (53km) from Welsh Frankton in Shropshire to Newtown in Powys, is gradually being restored. You may see narrowboats cruising along this section.

❺ Turn over bridge at Belan Locks, immediately dropping **L** to canal towpath. Head north along canal, later passing beneath main road. Entering Welshpool, remain on towpath, passing Powysland Museum and Montgomery Canal Centre (on opposite bank), with its exhibits of local agriculture, crafts and the canal and railway systems. Beyond short aqueduct and former railway bridge, climb out to road and turn **L** back to car park.

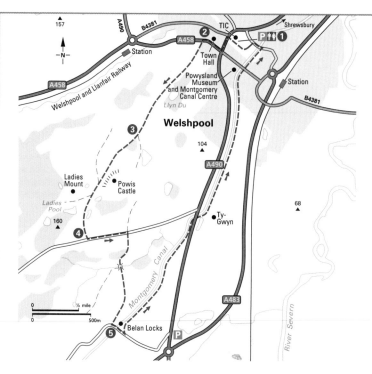

PISTYLL RHAEADR And Cadair Berwyn

This demanding, but short, walk brings magnificent views and spectacular waterfalls.

5 miles/8km 3hrs **Ascent** 1,870ft/570m ▲ **Difficulty** ③
Paths Well-defined paths and tracks, 7 stiles
Map OS Explorer 255 Llangollen & Berwyn **Grid ref** SJ 076293
Parking Car park 220yds (201m) before Tan-y-pistyll farm/café, where there's another pay car park

❶ From more easterly, and smaller, of 2 car parks turn **R** along road for about 400yds (366m), then turn sharp **L** to follow wide grassy track that climbs northwest to enter cwm of Nant y Llyn. At obvious fork keep **R** on rising track heading north towards crags of Cerrig Poethion.

❷ Track degenerates into path that traverses hillsides scattered with gorse. Higher up it crosses 2 streams before reaching Llyn Lluncaws in moss and heather cwm. Now path climbs south of lake and up shale and grass spur to **L** of Moel Sych's crags. Follow path along edge of crags on **R** to reach col between Moel Sych and Cadair Berwyn. From here climb to rocky south top of latter peak. Onward trip to trig point on Cadair Berwyn's lower north summit is straightforward but offers no advantages as viewpoint.

❸ From south top retrace your footsteps to col, but this time instead of tracing cliff edge now follow ridge

fence to cairn on Moel Sych summit plateau, crossing stile just before reaching it.

❹ Recross stile and turn **R** (south) to follow fence down wide, peaty spur cloaked with moor grass, mosses and little heather. Over slight rise, path descends again to stile (wobbly when checked) before dropping into high moorland cwm of the Disgynfa, where path is met by stony track that climbs from base of falls.

❺ To make there-and-back detour to top of falls, ignore stony track, but go through gate into forest and follow path to river. If not, descend along previously mentioned track, which zig-zags down before turning **R** to head for Tan-y-pistyll complex. Path to bottom of falls starts from café. It leads to footbridge across Afon Rhaeadr for best views.

❻ From café it's short walk along road to car park.

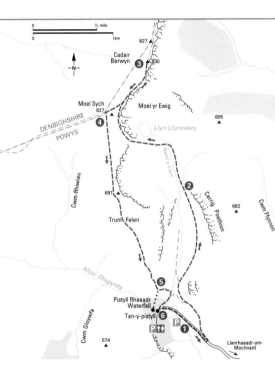

LLANBERIS The Long Way

A route on one of Snowdon's quieter ridges.

10 miles/16.1km 6hrs 30min **Ascent** 3,839ft/1,170m ⚠ **Difficulty** ③
Paths Well-defined paths and tracks, 1 stile
Map OS Explorer OL17 Snowdon **Grid ref** SH 577604
Parking Several car parks throughout Llanberis

❶ From the tourist information centre in Llanberis, head south along High Street (Stryd Fawr) before turning **R** up Capel Coch Road. Go ahead at junction, where road changes its name to Stryd Ceunant; continue past youth hostel and climb towards Braich y Foel, northeast spur of Moel Eilio.
❷ Where tarmac ends at foot of Moel Eilio, continue along track, which swings **L** (southeast) into wild cwm of the Afon Arddu.
❸ At base of Foel Goch's northern spur, Cefn Drum, track swings **R** into Maesgwm and climbs to pass named Bwlch Maesgwm, between Foel Goch and Moel Cynghorion. Go through gate, then turn **L** for steep climb by fence and up latter-mentioned peak.
❹ From Cynghorion's summit route descends along top of cliffs of Clogwyn Llechwedd Llo to another pass, Bwlch Cwm Brwynog, overlooking small reservoir of Llyn Ffynnon-y-gwas. Here join Snowdon Ranger Path.
❺ Follow zig-zag route up Clogwyn Du'r Arddu,

whose cliffs, on **L**, plummet to little tarn, Llyn Du'r Arddu, in dark stony cwm. Near top wide path veers **R**, away from edge, meets Snowdon Mountain Railway, and follows line to monolith at Bwlch Glas. Here you are met by both Llanberis Path and Pyg Track and look down on huge cwms of Glaslyn and Llyn Llydaw.
❻ Path now follows line of railway to summit. Retrace your steps to Bwlch Glas, but this time follow wide Llanberis Path on western slopes of Garnedd Ugain and above railway. (Don't mistake this for higher ridge path to Garnedd Ugain's summit.)
❼ Near Clogwyn Station come to Cwm Hetiau, where cliffs fall away into chasm of Pass of Llanberis. Path goes under railway and below Clogwyn Station before recrossing line near Halfway Station.
❽ Path meets lane beyond Hebron, and descends back into Llanberis near Royal Victoria Hotel. Turn **L** along main road, then take **L** fork, High Street, return to car.

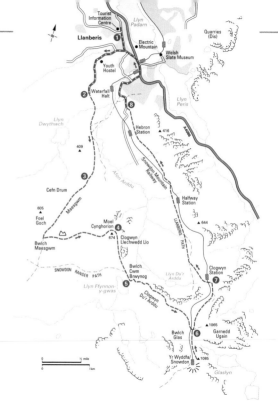

LLANSTUMDWY Lloyd George Country
Following the last Liberal Prime Minister.

6 miles/9.7km 4hrs **Ascent** 300ft/91m ⚠ **Difficulty** ①
Paths Generally well-defined paths and tracks, 4 stiles **Map** OS Explorer 254 Lleyn Peninsula East
Grid ref SH 476383 **Parking** Large car park at east end of village **NOTE** Small section of coast path engulfed by highest tides. Make sure you know times of tides before setting off

❶ Turn **R** from car park and go through past museum to bridge over Afon Dwyfor. Turn **R** along lane, then follow footpath on **L** past memorial and down to wooded riverbanks.
❷ After 1.5 miles (2.4km) path turns **R**, then goes under stone archway to meet tarred drive. Turn **L** along this, carry on to B4411 and turn **R**.
❸ After about 500yds (457m), turn **R** down enclosed drive. As another drive merges from **L**, turn half **L** along path shaded by rhododendrons. After few paces, go though kissing gate; cross field guided by fence on **L**. Through next kissing gate path veers half **R**, following fence now on **R**.
❹ Beyond gate now sketchy route cuts diagonally (southeast) across 2 fields to rejoin B4411, 1 mile (1.6km) or so north of Criccieth. Follow B4411 into town. Keep straight on at crossroads, and bear **L** after level crossing to reach promenade.

❺ Follow coast road past castle and continue until it turns firmly inland. From here, tide permitting, simply follow coast path or walk along sands. Otherwise, follow road to bridleway on **L**. Go past Muriau and then **R** of Ty Cerrig. Cross track and field then turn **R** on green track, nearly to railway. Head **L**, back to coast east of Ynysgain Fawr. Follow coast path west through coastal grasslands and gorse scrub to estuary of Dwyfor and crumbled sea defences.
❻ At metal kissing gate, waymarks point inland. Follow these, with fence on **R**. Route becomes farm track that cuts under railway and passes through yard of Aberkin farm before reaching main road.
❼ Cross main road with care and go through gate on opposite side. Short path leads to unsurfaced lane; follow to village centre. Turn **R** for car park.

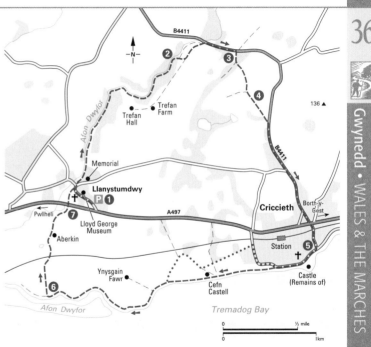

CNICHT Tackling The Knight

An exhilarating climb to one of the peaks.

6.5 miles/10.4km 4hrs 30min **Ascent** 2,297ft/700m ⚠ **Difficulty** ③
Paths Mostly well-defined, but sketchy by Bwlch y Battel, 9 stiles
Map OS Explorer OL17 Snowdon **Grid ref** SH 634485
Parking Parking area near Gelli-lago

❶ Walk south along road then turn **L** along track to Gelli-lago (Nantmor Mountain Centre). Go through gate to **L** of house then round **R** behind it to footbridge. Stony path now winds up hillside, with stream on **L** and Cnicht appearing on horizon ahead.

❷ After more level stretch, path veers **R** and climbs to ladder stile and wild pass of Bwlch y Battel. Path peters out, but marshy passage between high rocky hillsides keeps you on straight and narrow. Descend towards tarn and pass above and **L** of it. Descend by its outlet stream through valley to marshy hollow. Bear **R** on clearer path and descend little more to meet broader path, main Croesor to Cnicht route.

❸ Double back to **L** on main path and climb on to narrowing south ridge of Cnicht, which leads you to the summit.

❹ Continue northeast, overlooking Llyn Biswail on **L** and Llyn Cwm-y-foel on **R**, to reach col overlooking large tarn, Llyn yr Adar.

❺ Descend **L** to traverse marshy grasslands east of tarn. Path veers **L** beyond northern shores before swinging **R** to cross low notch and then follow grassy shelf in rocks of Y Cyrniau. Descend into bouldery hollow.

❻ Follow stream down, ignoring small path to **R**, until main path becomes clearer, overlooking Llyn Llagi. Follow path down over rough moorland and pasture, staying roughly parallel to outlet stream of llyn. Finally descend, closer to stream, to stile just above Llwynyrhwch farm, with its tall pine tree.

❼ Pass in front of farm then go diagonally **R** across fields to cottage. Go over rise to road and turn **L**, back to car park.

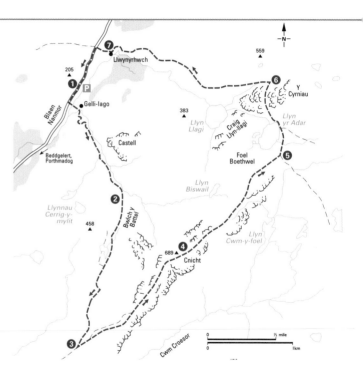

ABERGLASLYN Copper In The Hills

A walk up to the old copper mines.

4 miles/6.4km 2hrs 30min **Ascent** 1,181ft/360m ⚠ **Difficulty** ③

Paths Well-maintained paths and tracks (see note below), 2 stiles **Map** OS Explorer OL17 Snowdon
Grid ref SH 597462 **Parking** National Trust pay car park, Aberglaslyn
NOTE Short section of riverside path in Aberglaslyn gorge is difficult and requires use of handholds

❶ Path starts to **L** of toilet block and goes under old railway bridge, before climbing through Cwm Bychan. After steady climb path reaches iron pylons of aerial cableway.

❷ Beyond pylons, keep straight on, ignoring paths forking **L**. Grassy corridor leads to col, where there's a stile in fence that is not shown on maps. Bear **L** beyond stile and head for 3-way footpath signpost by rocks of Grib Ddu.

❸ Follow path on **L** signed 'To Beddgelert and Sygun' and cross ladder stile. Turn **L**, then follow path down round rocky knoll and then down hillside to signpost. Just beyond sign is cairn at Bwlch-y-Sygyn and over to **L** is shallow, peaty pool in green hollow.

❹ Path now heads southwest along mountain's northwestern ridge, overlooking Beddgelert. Ignore lesser paths along way.

❺ Watch out for large cairn, highlighting turn-off **R** for Beddgelert. Clear stony path weaves through

rhododendron and rock, goes through kissing gate in wall half-way down, then descends further to edge of Beddgelert, where little lane passing cottage of Penlan leads to Afon Glaslyn.

❻ Turn **L** to follow river for short way. Don't cross footbridge over river but turn **L** to follow Glaslyn's east bank. Cross restored railway line and then continue between it and river.

❼ Below 1st tunnel, path is pushed **R** to water's edge. Handholds screwed into rocks assist passage on difficult but short section. Path continues through riverside woodland and over boulders until it comes to Pont Aberglaslyn.

❽ Here, turn **L** up steps and follow dirt path through woods. Just before railway, follow signed path down and **R** to car park.

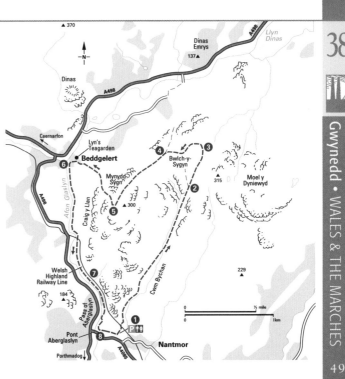

ROMAN STEPS With The Drovers
Along one of Snowdonia's oldest highways.

7 miles/11.3km 5hrs **Ascent** 1,575ft/480m ⚠ **Difficulty** ③
Paths Rocky paths, tracks and boggy moorland, 9 stiles
Map OS Explorer OL18 Harlech, Porthmadog & Bala **Grid ref** SH 646314 **Parking** Llyn Cwm Bychan
NOTE The moorlands around the eastern end of the walk can be very wet and dangerous, with streams under the bogland. The walk is best tackled after a long dry spell

❶ Exit gate at back of car park and over paved causeway across stream. Beyond stile path climbs up through squat woodland.

❷ Over another stile leave woodland and cross stream on small bridge. Clear path climbs steadily to gate. Now slabbed with 'steps', it climbs through heather-clad rocky ravine and on to cairn marking highest point along rocky pass of Bwlch Tyddiad.

❸ From col, path descends into grassy moorland basin beneath Rhinog Fawr, then, beyond stile, enters conifers of Coed-y-Brenin plantation. Well-defined footpath tucks away under trees and eventually reaches wide flinted forestry road; turn **L** on this.

❹ After about 1 mile (1.6 km), road swings away to head east; watch out for waymarked path on **L** just beyond turn. Waymarks guide route **L**, then **R**, to pass ruins of Hafod-Gynfal. Beyond this head north to cross ladder stile and out of forest.

❺ Go straight ahead from stile, heading north across grassy moor of Moel y Gwartheg. Ground gets wet as you descend, but it's wetter still further **R**. Head for isolated cottage of Wern-fach, little to **L** of conifers, but for now aim towards green fields of Cefn Clawdd.

❻ Meet fence, which guides you to Wern-fâch. Cross stile, then just above cottage turn **L** and go over 2 ladder stiles. Follow main stream (Afon Crawcwellt) to Wern-cyfrdwy (house), pass behind it, then join walls and fences that shadow stream. These give least wet line across sodden moorland.

❼ Going firms up as ground steepens, climbing to lonely col of Bwlch Gwylim, narrow pass between Clip and Craig Wion. Descending far side, Cwm Bychan and start of walk come back into view. Footpath now descends to southwest, through heather and bracken. After ladder stile, look for small waymark; turn **L** down steep slopes back to car park.

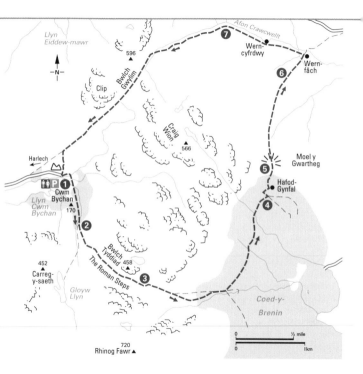

NANTCOL High Lakes And Highwaymen
Wild Nantcol and a lake between two peaks.

5.5 miles/8.8km 3hrs 30min **Ascent** 1,378ft/420m ⚠ **Difficulty** ③
Paths Peaty paths through heather and farm tracks, 1 stile
Map OS Explorer OL18 Harlech, Porthmadog & Bala **Grid ref** SH 633259
Parking Small fee for parking at Cil-cychwyn farm or Maes-y-garnedd

❶ From farm at Cil-cychwyn, follow narrow lane up valley to its end. Here continue on narrow wall-side path, initially hidden, through upper Nantcol. Path traverses lower south flanks of Rhinog Fawr before entering dark pass of Bwlch Drws-Ardudwy.
❷ In marshy basin beneath Rhinog Fawr and Rhinog Fach look for ladder stiles over wall on **R**. 1st leads to very steep short-cut that bypasses Llyn Cwmhosan. Preferably, take 2nd stile to narrow path climbing through heather and passing west shores of Llyn Cwmhosan, and beneath boulder and screes of Rhinog Fach's west face. Beyond this, route reaches shores of Llyn Hywel.
❸ For best views take path **L** of farm, crossing bouldery screes, and to top of huge Y Llethr Slabs, that plummet into lake. You could do a complete circuit of Llyn Hywel, but this would mean climbing much higher up slopes of Y Llethr. It is much easier to retrace

your steps to lake's outlet point, then continue along west shore.
❹ Turn **R** to follow sketchy narrow path down to Llyn Perfeddau which is soon visible. Nearing lake, keep straight ahead on faint path where clearer path goes **R**.
❺ Follow wall running behind lake then, after about 0.5 mile (800m), go though gap in wall to follow grassy path that rounds rocky knoll high above Nantcol before passing old mine. Descend **L** to prominent track that winds past mine workings before adopting straighter course, passing ruined farm.
❻ Through woodland and high pasture, track passes Graig-Isaf farm to reach valley road at Cil-cychwyn.

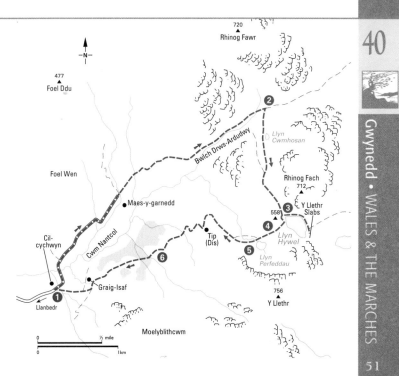

BARMOUTH The Sublime Mawddach

Follow in the illustrious footsteps of Wordsworth, Darwin and Ruskin on this lovely watery walk.

6 miles/9.7km 4hrs **Ascent** 656ft/200m ⚠ **Difficulty** 2
Paths A bridge, good tracks and woodland paths, 6 stiles
Map OS Explorer OL23 Cadair Idris & Llyn Tegid **Grid ref** SH 613155
Parking Car park on seafront

❶ Follow promenade round harbour, then go over footbridge across estuary (toll). On reaching path along south shore of estuary, turn **L** to follow grassy embankment that leads to track rounding wooded knoll of Fegla Fawr on its seaward side.

❷ Reaching terraced houses of Mawddach Crescent, follow track that passes to their rear. Rejoin track along shoreline until you reach gate on **R** marking start of bridleway heading inland across marshes of Arthog.

❸ Turn **L** along old railway track, then leave it just before crossing of little Arthog Estuary and turn **R** along tarmac lane by small car park. Bear **L** over ladder stile and follow raised embankment to wall which now leads path to main Dolgellau road next to St Catherine's Church.

❹ Opposite church gate is footpath beginning with steps into woodland. Good waymarked path now climbs by Arthog.

❺ Beyond stile at top of woods, turn **R** to come to lane. Turn **R** along descending lane, then **L** along stony track passing cottage (Merddyn). Track gets narrower and steeper as it descends into more woodland, beneath boulders of old quarry and down to Dolgellau road by Arthog Village Hall.

❻ Turn **R** along road, then **L** along path back to railway track and Mawddach Trail. Turn **L** along trail and follow it past Morfa Mawddach Station and back across Barmouth's bridge.

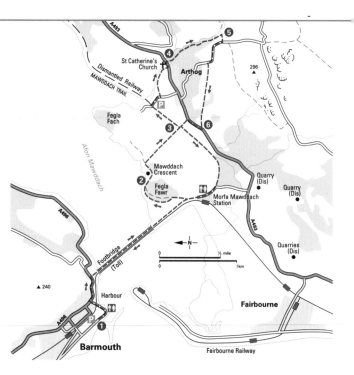

PRECIPICE WALK On The Edge

A balcony route with spectacular views of valley, mountain and estuary.

3 miles/4.8km 2hrs **Ascent** Negligible ⚠ **Difficulty** 1
Paths Stony tracks and good paths, occasionally rough, 4 stiles
Map OS Explorer OL18 Harlech, Porthmadog & Bala **Grid ref** SH 745211
Parking Coed y Groes car park on Dolgellau–Llanfachreth road **NOTE** Wear strong footwear as part of route follows narrow path with big drops down to Mawddach Valley. Not a walk for vertigo sufferers

❶ From top end of car park turn **R** on level footpath which curves around to join another wide track. The Precipice Walk is a private path around the Nannau Estate, but its use has been authorised by the estate owners since 1890, on the basis that all walkers observe the country code. It's probably one of the finest short routes in Wales and, as such, has been one of Dolgellau's most famous attractions since those early days when Victorian tourists came for their constitutional perambulations. Track swings **R** at edge of fields.

❷ Where track comes to estate cottage, Gwern-offeiriaid, turn **L** off it. Follow clear path leading to hillside north of Llyn Cynwch. There you see the grand mansion of Nannau, built for the Vaughans in 1796.

❸ At footpath signpost fork **R**. Path climbs hillside and turns northwards by side of dry-stone wall.

❹ Beyond stile footpath curves around crag-studded hill, with open slopes that give fine views across green valley below to village of Llanfachreth and rugged mountainsides of Rhobell Fawr and Dduallt that lie behind. Footpath edges rounds Foel Cynwch and passes Sitka spruce woodlands of Coed Dôl-y-clochydd. Ignore path signed to Glasdir and keep **L**, reaching dramatic, but even ledge path traversing high hill slopes above Mawddach Valley. Where slopes finally ease, there's promontory on **R**, with bench placed to enjoy view. Path now arcs round to southern side of Foel Faner, drops to lake and turns sharp **L** to follow western shore.

❺ Path meets outward route by hill footpath sign. Retrace outward route past estate cottage of Gwern-offeiriaid and through woods back to car park.

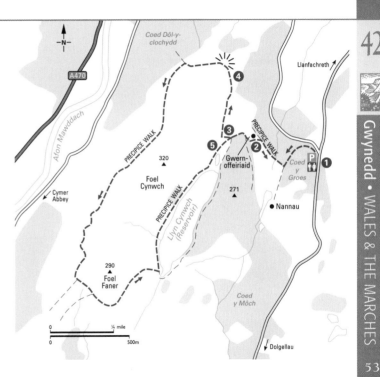

BALA A View Of Bala's Lake
The best view of Wales' largest natural lake.

5 miles/8km 3hrs **Ascent** 656ft/200m ⚠ **Difficulty** 2
Paths Woodland and field paths, 7 stiles
Map OS Explorer OL23 Cadair Idris & Llyn Tegid, or OS Explorer OL18 Harlech, Porthmadog and Bala
Grid ref SH 929361 **Parking** Car park at entrance to Bala town from east

❶ Go to north corner of car park to access riverside path. Turn **R** to follow raised embankment along west bank of Tryweryn. After dog-leg to **R**, passing through 2 kissing gates, footpath continues, first by banks of Tryweryn, then by north banks of Dee.

❷ At road, cross bridge over River Dee, then smaller, older bridge. Go through kissing gate to cross small field to Bala Station on Bala Lake Railway. Footbridge allows you to cross track before traversing 2 small fields.

❸ Turn **R** along cart track, and continue to pass behind Bala Lake Hotel. Waymarker points direction up grassy bank on **L**, and path continues to stile and then follows fence on **R**.

❹ Descend slightly to cross stream beside small cottage, go up again then along level fence to stile. Bear **L** up through bracken and wind up steeply at first, then continue more easily to tarmac lane.

❺ Turn **L** along lane to cattle grid from where you continue on stony track, passing through felled plantations.

❻ Just before isolated house (Cefn-ddwygraig), turn **L** off track to ladder stile. Follow grooved grass track across gorse-covered slopes. Keep **L** at fork and then drop down to stile. Well-waymarked path continues north, with Bala town ahead.

❼ Go over partially hidden step stile into commercial forestry plantations of Coed Pen-y-bont. Narrow footpath descends to bottom edge of woods (ignore forestry track you meet on way down).

❽ At bottom of woods turn **R** along track that reaches road by Pen-y-Bont Campsite. Turn **L** along road, cross Dee again, bear **L** and then follow lakeside footpath past information centre. At main road, turn **R** to explore town centre.

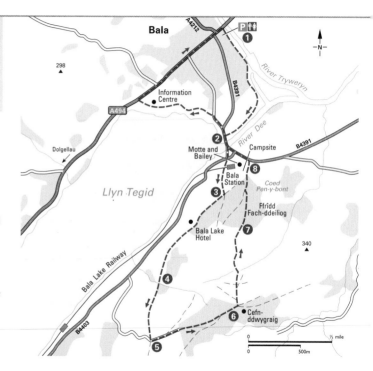

THE DYSYNNI VALLEY Castell Y Bere

Exploring the valleys where the Welsh princes held out against the might of Edward I.

5 miles/8km 3hrs **Ascent** 656ft/200m ▲ **Difficulty** 2
Paths Field paths and tracks, 14 stiles
Map OS Explorer OL23 Cadair Idris & Llyn Tegid **Grid ref** SH 677069
Parking Car park by community centre in Abergynolwyn

❶ Cross road to Railway Inn and take lane ('Llanegryn'). At far side of bridge spanning Dysynni river, turn **R** through kissing gate and trace above north banks. At 2nd step stile path turns **L** before climbing steps alongside tall leylandii to country lane.
❷ Turn **R** along lane which heads east through Dysynni Valley and beneath woodlands of Coed Meriafel. At junction with B4405 turn **L**, over stile and climb northwest across field. Continue over 2 more stiles to woodland path. Follow this to forestry track near top of woods.
❸ Turn **L** along track which climbs out of woods before veering **R** to gate and adjacent stile, giving entry into large field. Go ahead to pick up ruined overgrown wall. Where this ends, bear **L** to descend high grassy cwm with stream developing just to **L**. Ford another stream which joins from **R** near ruin.
❹ Green path develops flinted surface. Leave it as it starts to climb and rejoin streamside path on **L**. This descends into woods and stays close to stream. After passing cascades it comes out of woods to reach track, which in turn leads to road at Llanfihangel-y-pennant opposite chapel.
❺ Turn **L** past chapel and Castell y Bere (detour through gates on **R** for closer look). Just beyond castle, take path on **L** that climbs to gate at top **R-H** corner of field. Turn **R** along green track which passes Caerberllan farm to come to road. Turn **R**, go **L** at crossroads and cross Pont Ystumanner (bridge).
❻ Now footpath signpost highlights track on **L**, which passes below Rhiwlas farm and continues as green path above river. Path eases across slopes of Gamallt and swings **L** with valley.
❼ Beyond river gorge, path approaches back of Abergynolwyn and turns **L** to cross old iron bridge across river. Turn **R** along unsurfaced street to return to village centre.

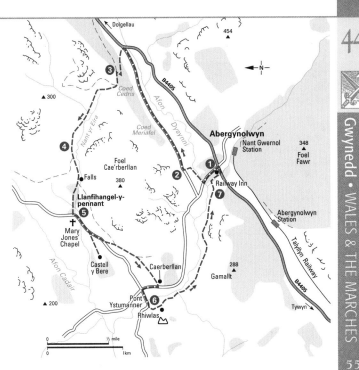

45

HOLYHEAD MOUNTAIN Last Stop Before Ireland
Rugged and rocky Holy Island offers some of the best walking in Anglesey.

5 miles/8km 3hrs **Ascent** 1,230ft/375m ⚠ **Difficulty** ☑ 2
Paths Well-maintained paths and tracks
Map OS Explorer 262 Anglesey West **Grid ref** SH 210818
Parking RSPB car park

❶ Take path for RSPB centre at Ellin's Tower, small white castellated building, then climb along path back to road which should be followed to its end.
❷ If you're not visiting South Stack Lighthouse, climb **R** on path passing stone shelter. Path detours **R** to round BT aerials and dishes. At crossroads go **L**, heading back to coast, then take **L** fork. Ignore next **L** (dead end path) and continue following waymarks over north shoulder of Holyhead Mountain.
❸ Ignore paths leading off **R** to summit, but keep **L** on good path heading north towards North Stack.
❹ After passing through grassy walled enclosure path descends in zig-zags down steep slopes. Joining track follow it **L** to rocky platform, where Fog Signal Station and island of North Stack come into full view. Retrace steps up zig-zags and towards Holyhead Mountain.
❺ At junction below summit path, turn sharp **L** across heath. Go **R** at its end, contouring eastern side of mountain. Keep **R** at fork and ignore another

summit path from **R**. Beyond mountain, take **R** fork as path comes to wall. Follow path downhill towards rough pastureland.
❻ Go down grassy walled track before turning **R** along similar one. This soon becomes rough path traversing more heathland, now to south of Holyhead Mountain.
❼ Where waymarked path is later signed off **L**, bear **R** below craggy cliffs towards relay station. Go **L** at far end but just before meeting outward route, swing **L** again on another path past radio masts. Approaching service track, bear **L** again on to tarmac path. Continue with it over stile beside gate, emerging at end on to road opposite café.
❽ Turn **L** to return to car park.

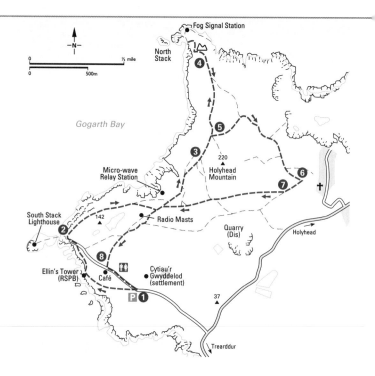

MOELFRE The Ancient Village

Walk along Anglesey's beautiful east coast to discover a remarkably intact ancient village.

5 miles/8km 3hrs **Ascent** 541ft/165m ⚠ **Difficulty** ☐1

Paths Well-defined coastal and field paths, 5 stiles

Map OS Explorer 263 Anglesey East **Grid ref** SH 511862

Parking Car park at entrance to village

❶ From car park, follow main road (A5108) down to shore. Road winds behind bay before swinging **L**. Leave road at that point for shoreline path on **R**.

❷ Pass Seawatch Centre and lifeboat station and ignore footpath signs pointing inland. Instead follow clear coast path that looks across to island of Ynys Moelfre. After passing to **R** of terraced cottages and going through couple of kissing gates path crosses small caravan site. It then goes through another kissing gate and climbs past Royal Charter memorial.

❸ Swinging **L** into Porth Forllwyd, path ends beside cottage, Moryn. Follow track to gate, turning before it along fenced path into field. Keep ahead to rejoin coast, which turns in above large bay of Traeth Lligwy.

❹ On reaching beach car park, turn **L** along narrow lane before going straight ahead at next crossroads.

❺ Take next path on **R**, signposted to Din Lligwy ancient village. First, turn half **R** across field to see old chapel. Then bear **L** across 2 fields and into wood

concealing Din Lligwy. Return to lane and turn **R** along it.

❻ Leave after 50yds (46m) over ladder stile on **L**. Follow doglegging boundary **R** to stile, over which turn **L**, walking downfield to emerge by roadside quarry at Aber-strecht.

❼ Follow lane **R** to edge of village and go **L** on waymarked track. Around 1st bend, swing **L** through gate, keeping **R** at fork to walk through caravan site again.

❽ Follow shoreline path back to start.

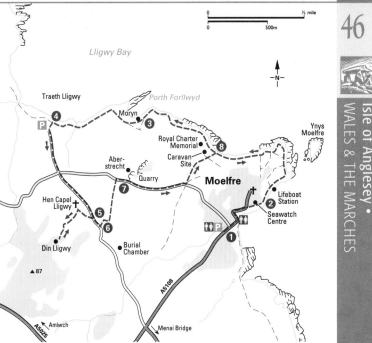

CAPEL CURIG An Alpine Journey

Discovering the valley where the rocks and mountains provide challenging ground for today's climbers and mountaineers.

4 miles/6.4km 2hrs **Ascent** 295ft/90m ⚠ **Difficulty** 2
Paths Generally clear and surfaced but can be wet in places, 9 stiles
Map OS Explorer OL17 Snowdon **Grid ref** SJ 720582 **Parking** Behind Joe Brown's shop at Capel Curig

❶ Path begins at ladder stile by war memorial on A5 and climbs towards Y Pincin, large craggy outcrop cloaked in wood and bracken. Cross another stile and keep to **L** of outcrop. Those who want to go to the top should do so from the northeast, where the gradients are easier. It's fun, but take care! You'll need to retrace your steps to the main route.

❷ Continue east through woods and across marshy ground, keeping well **R** of great crags of Clogwynmawr. At 2 ladder stiles, ignore footpath, **R**, back down to road, but maintain direction across hillside.

❸ Just beyond footbridge over Nant y Geuallt, leave main footpath and follow less well-defined one, with marker posts, across marshy ground. Path veers southeast to cross another stream before coming to prominent track.

❹ Turn **R** along track, go over ladder stile, then at 4-way meeting of paths head **L**. Follow path

descending into woods. Take **R-H** fork descending to road near Ty'n y Coed Inn.

❺ Turn **L** down road, then **R**, along lane over Pont-Cyfyng. Go **R** again beyond bridge to follow footpath that traces Llugwy to another bridge opposite Cobdens Hotel. Don't cross this time, but scramble **L** over rocks before continuing through woods of Coed Bryn-engan, where path soon becomes wide track.

❻ After passing cottage (Bryn-engan), track comes to bridge at head of Mymbyr lakes. Turn **R** across it, then go **L** along road for short way.

❼ Cross road to next ladder stile and take track straight ahead, soon swinging **R** to hug foot of southern Glyder slopes.

❽ Beyond Gelli farm turn **R** to follow cart track back to car park.

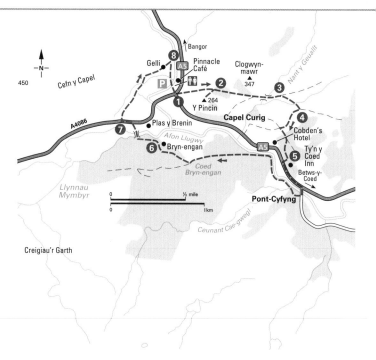

OGWEN The Devil's Kitchen

Explore the most perfect hanging valley in Snowdonia – its rock ledges and hanging valleys.

3 miles/4.8km 2hrs 30min **Ascent** 1,378ft/420m **Difficulty** 2
Paths Well-defined paths
Map OS Explorer OL17 Snowdon **Grid ref** SH 649603
Parking Small pay car park at Ogwen; others along Llyn Ogwen

1 Cwm Idwal nature trail starts to **L** of toilet block at Ogwen and climbs up hillside to pass impressive waterfalls before turning **R** and continuing up hill.

2 Go through gate in fence, that marks boundary of National Nature Reserve, and turn **L** along side of Llyn Idwal's eastern shores. Clear footpath climbs into dark shadows of Cwm Idwal.

3 Now leave nature trail, which turns **R** to complete circuit around lake. Instead ascend beneath rock climbing grounds of Idwal Slabs and across stream of Nant Ifan, beyond which footpath zig-zags up rough boulder ground to foot of Twll Du – Devil's Kitchen. If weather, and the forecast too, are fine climb to Llyn y Cwn at top of this impressive defile, if not, skip this bit and go to Point **6**.

4 To ascend Twll Du climb engineered path as it angles **L** up rock face, which will now be on **R-H** side, above extensive area of scree and boulder. At top reach relatively gentle (by comparison) grassy hollow

between rising summits of Y Garn, to **R**, and Glyder Fawr, to **L**.

5 Just beyond 1st grassy mounds is small tarn of Llyn y Cwn – dog lake – which makes great picnic spot. Now retrace steps carefully to bottom of Twll Du.

6 Among huge boulders, path forks and **L** branch heads down to run above western shore of Llyn Idwal, then rounds its northern end to meet outward route at Point **2**. Now follow route of your outward journey back to car park at Ogwen.

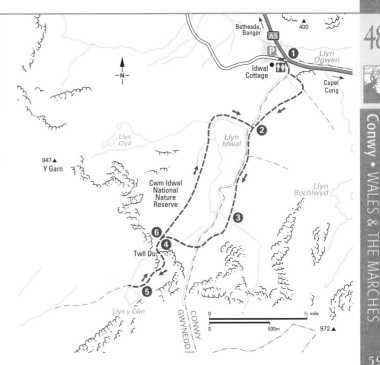

LLYN CRAFNANT The Twin Lakes

Discover two lakes, one to inspire poets present and one that inspired bards past.

5 miles/8km 3hrs **Ascent** 984ft/300m ▲ **Difficulty** 2
Paths Clear paths and forestry tracks, 5 stiles
Map OS Explorer OL17 Snowdon **Grid ref** SH 756618
Parking Forestry pay car park, north of Llyn Crafnant

❶ Turn **R** out of car park and follow lane to north end of Llyn Crafnant. Turn **R** again here, and follow forestry track along northwest shores of lake, before taking lower **L** fork.

❷ Ignore stile on **L**, and instead climb with forestry track. Keep watching for later waymarked footpath on which you should descend **L** to cross stream by cottage (Hendre Bach). Turn **L** down track passing 2 modern chalets.

❸ Turn **L** along road which heads back towards lake. Leave this at telephone box for path, signposted 'Llyn Geirionydd' and waymarked with blue-capped posts. This climbs through conifer forests and overshoulder of Mynydd Deulyn.

❹ Descend with main winding forestry track, still following obvious blue-capped posts. Ignore track forking to **R** – it leads to Llyn Bychan.

❺ On reaching valley floor, leave track to go over step stile on **L**. Path crosses couple of meadows

beneath Ty-newydd cottage before tracing Llyn Geirionydd's shoreline. At northern end of lake path keeps to **R** of wall and meets farm track.

❻ Turn **L** and immediately **R** to Taliesin Monument on grassy mound. Descend to green path heading north towards Crafnant Valley.

❼ Veer **L** to cross ladder stile and follow undulating path ahead over wooded rock and heather knolls.

❽ Path eventually swings **L** to reach old mine. Here, take lower track on **R** which descends back to valley road and forest car park.

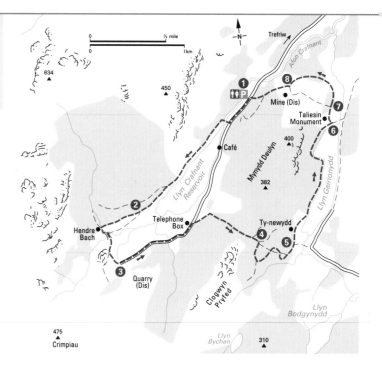

DOLGARROG Tragic Disaster Area

Discovering grim secrets, high in one of the Carneddau's loneliest valleys.

7 miles/11.3km 3hrs 30min **Ascent** 500ft/152m ⚠ **Difficulty** ☐1

Paths Tracks and country lanes, 5 stiles
Map OS Explorer OL17 Snowdon **Grid ref** SH 731663
Parking Car park at the end of road

❶ Follow track heading roughly southwest from car park into jaws of Eigiau. This turns **L** below main dam and goes over bridge across reservoir's outflow stream.
❷ Turn **L** along greener track that runs above and parallel to river, ignoring path on **R** beneath Eilio. Gated track passes Coedty Reservoir and then leads to country lane by the dam.
❸ Follow lane as it descends to cross river, then climbs out on to hillside high above Conwy Valley.
❹ Turn **L** at T-junction to Rowlyn Isaf farm. Quickest and recommended route follows quiet country lane back to car park.

An Alternative Route

It is possible to get back by using path south of Waen Bryn-gwenith. However it's very rough in early stages where path is lost in thick bracken. For purist however signposted path from wood, beyond farm climbs beside wall and fades near top end of woods. Here look out for small gate on **L**. Now you have to fight through thick bracken (easier in winter) to reach next field where you find gate beside ruin. Go **L**, then follow contours round **R**, and keep above longitudinal fence/wall. Nearing road, cross ladder stile then turn **R** to another one by road. Turn **L** along road to start.

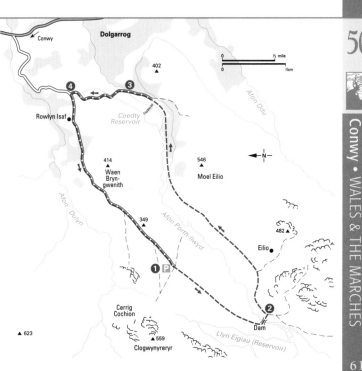

CONWY Castle Stronghold
Conwy's castle and a remote Celtic fort.

6.75 miles/10.9km 4hrs **Ascent** 1,493ft/455m ⚠ **Difficulty** 2
Paths Good paths and easy-to-follow moorland tracks, 5 stiles
Map OS Explorer OL17 Snowdon **Grid ref** SH 783775
Parking Large car park on Llanrwst Road behind Conwy Castle

1 From Conwy Quay head northwest along waterfront, past Smallest House and under town walls. Fork **R** along tarmac waterside footpath that rounds Bodlondeb Wood. Turn **L** along road, past school and on to A547. Cross road, then railway line by footbridge. Track beyond skirts wood to reach lane; turn **R**.
2 At fork bear **R** past house to waymarked stile, from which footpath rakes up wooded hillsides up on to Conwy Mountain. Follow undulating crest of Conwy Mountain and continue past Castell Caer.
3 Several tracks converge in high fields of Pen-Pyra. Follow signposts for North Wales Path along track heading to southwest over **L** shoulder of Alltwen and down to metalled road traversing Sychnant Pass.
4 Follow footpath from other side of road, skirting woods on **L**. Over stile carry on past Gwern Engen to meet track. Go **R** and then bear **L**, dropping above lodge to reach lane. Turn **R** along lane, then turn **L** at next junction, into Groesffordd. Cross road, then take

road ahead that swings to **R** past telephone box, then **L** (southeast) towards Plas Iolyn.
5 Turn **L** at end; leave opposite white house on path climbing to cottage. Cross track and continue upfield to B5106. Go **L** to Conwy Touring Park. Follow drive to hairpin, from which waymarked path climbs through trees, recrossing drive. Finally emerging through kissing gate, continue up field edge. Swing **L** along undulating ridge above successive pastures, finally meeting lane.
6 Turn **L**, shortly leaving **R** along track past communications mast to Bryn-locyn. Continue at edge of fields beyond to stile by Coed Benarth, from which path drops beside wood.
7 Go over adder stile on **L-H** side and descend field to roadside gate at bottom. Turn **R** on to B5106 to return to quayside, or turn **L** to get back to main car park.

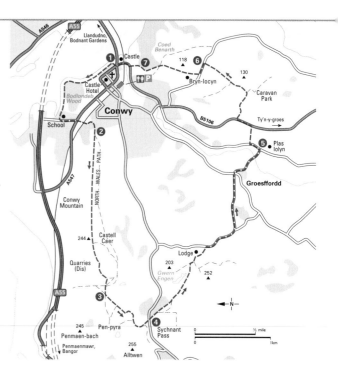

TAL Y FAN Stones And Settlements

Visit the most northerly 2,000ft (610m) hill in Wales and see what remains from ancient settlers.

5 miles/8km 3hrs **Ascent** 984ft/300m ⚠ **Difficulty** 2
Paths Cart tracks and narrow mountain paths, 7 stiles
Map OS Explorer OL17 Snowdon **Grid ref** SH 720715
Parking Car park at end of Bwlch y Ddeufaen road, off B5106 Conwy–Llanwrst road

❶ From car park at top of metalled section of road to Bwlch y Ddeufaen, continue along road, which is now unsurfaced, and follow it past ancient standing stones to high pass itself, and go through gate in crossing wall.

❷ Turn **R** and follow course of wall, across pass under 3 lines of electricity pylons, and then up steep rocky slopes of Foel Lwyd. Narrow footpath continues, first descending to little saddle, or col, then climbing to even rockier summit of Tal y Fan.

❸ Descending footpath still follows line of drystone wall, but stays with more even ground on **L**. When wall turns **R**, continue ahead, towards prominent hill of Craig Celynin. Thread between outcrops to little green valley running down to **R**, where you look for gorse-covered mound (Caer Bach Fort).

❹ When you reach fort remains turn **R** to follow tumbled down wall heading southwest across high pastureland overlooking Conwy Valley. Except for short stretch this wall now acts as your guide, as do frequent

ladder stiles and locked gates in all intervening cross-walls on route.

❺ Footpath becomes cart track, which passes beneath whitewashed cottage (Cae Coch) before turning **L** to join stony vehicle track that has come from Rowen Youth Hostel.

❻ Turn **R** along track, which soon joins Bwlch y Ddeufaen road at sharp corner. Go straight ahead along road and follow it back to car park.

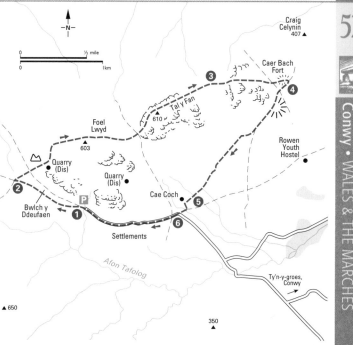

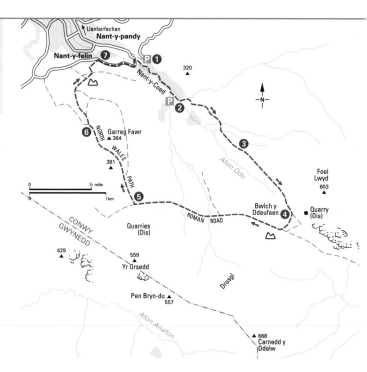

53

NANT-Y-COED Pass Of The Two Stones

A walk through one of the prettiest woods in Wales, to a high mountain pass.

5 miles/8km 3hrs **Ascent** 1,214ft/370m ⚠ **Difficulty** ☐2

Paths Woodland, field and moorland paths, cart tracks, 5 stiles

Map OS Explorer OL17 Snowdon **Grid ref** SH 694739

Parking Small car park on Newry Drive, Nant-y-pandy, Llanfairfechan

❶ Go through gate beyond car park and follow stony path through woods of Nant-y-Coed by stream. Take more prominent **L** fork up past pond, then cross stream using stepping stones. More stepping stones are used to cross side stream before climbing to 2nd car park.

❷ Signpost points way up valley and you cross footbridge by ford to continue. Keep sharp eye open for stone waymarks, which guide you through complex series of criss-crossing tracks.

❸ Path enters open moorland, still with occasional slate waymarks. Finally, ignore waymark that points **R** where track continues straight ahead. When path degenerates direct line is close to steeper rocky slopes on **L**. Aim for col between Foel Lwyd and Drosgl, point where 3 lines of pylons straddle fells.

❹ At Bwlch y Ddeufaen faint path arcs **R**, parallel to wall, to join Roman road. Turn **R** along track.

❺ At crossroads of tracks, turn **R** along one signposted 'Llanfairfechan' joining waymarked course of North Wales Path over Garreg Fawr. After 1st grassy summit path veers **L** to rake down west side of hill to wall.

❻ Take waymarked **R-H** fork rather than track following wall down **L**. Ignore narrow path forking **R**. Main track then threads **R** and descends steeply through pastures overlooking Nant-y-Coed. Turn **L** down little enclosed ginnel to road.

❼ Turn **R** along road, which rises then descends to bridge over Afon Llanfairfechan. At other side take narrow lane back to car park.

MYNYDD Y GAER With The Poet

Visit an Iron Age fort and look down on the magnificent land- and seascapes that inspired the 19th-century Jesuit priest and poet, Gerard Manley Hopkins.

3.25 miles/5.2km 2hrs **Ascent** 656ft/200m ⚠ **Difficulty** 2
Paths Field paths and tracks, 1 stile **Map** OS Explorer 264 Vale of Clwyd **Grid ref** SH 981706
Parking Llannefydd village car park

❶ Turn **L** out of car park and follow lane signposted to Llanfair TH (TH standing for Talhaiarn). Where road comes in from **L**, go though gate on **R-H** side and traverse fields with hedge and fence on **L**.
❷ Beyond gate in far corner, turn **L** with hedge, continuing uphill in 2nd field and then over stile. Leave through gate at top, winding out of small enclosure onto lane by Ochor-y-gaer. Turn **L**.
❸ Whereroad turns sharply to **L**, leave it and double-back to **R** on tarmac track climbing up to Bryn Hwylfa. Just past whitewashed cottage, turn **L** along enclosed grass track climbing hill. Beyond gate grassy footpath winds through gorse and scrub before veering **L** beneath outer ring defences of Iron Age fort.
❹ Where gorse bushes become more sparse, climb **R** to reach brow of hill. Go through farm gate to cairn at summit. Descend north from here, to pick up track that passes hilltop farm, Ty-newydd, before descending **L** to meet another lane.

❺ Turn **L** along lane, but leave it at **R-H** bend for grass track continuing ahead to pass above shores of Plâs-uchaf Reservoir. Past lake, track swings **L** towards Sychnant.
❻ Beyond gate track becomes path, winding through woodland before coming to lane that you left on outward route. Turn **R** along lane then 1st **L**, heading straight back to Llannefydd.

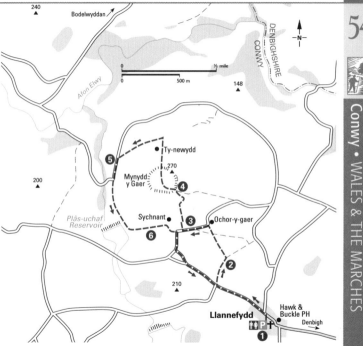

HORSESHOE FALLS The Velvet Hill

This walk on the Velvet Hill is probably one of the prettiest walks in North Wales.

3.5 miles/5.6km 2hrs **Ascent** 902ft/275m **Difficulty** 2
Paths Field paths in valley and on hillside, 10 stiles
Map OS Explorer 255 Llangollen & Berwyn **Grid ref** SJ 198433
Parking Picnic site and car park at Llantysilio Green on minor road north of Berwyn Station

❶ From car park walk down to road, turn **R** for few paces then descend steps to back of Chain Bridge Hotel. Turn **R** to follow path between river and canal. Through kissing gate at end of canal traverse riverside fields past Horseshoe Falls and climb to Llantysilio church. On reaching road, turn **L** through hamlet of Llantysilio to junction.

❷ Continue few paces further to find stile on **R** and then climb along rutted track, which keeps forest to **L**, then climbs north on high pastured hillside.

❸ Over stile at top of field path swings **R** above plantation. Keep **R** at fork and later cross stile before eventually descending to cottages at Pen-y-bryn. Enclosed path drops to stile, which leads out to Horseshoe Pass road at Britannia Inn.

❹ Turn **R** along road, then **R** again when you get to 1st junction. At bend, mount stile on **L** to head south across fields. Reaching farm track briefly go **R**, leaving

at fork over stile on **L** on to narrow lane. Go **L** here to meet Horseshoe Pass road again.

❺ Go over stile on **R-H** side of road, signposted to Velvet Hill, and ascend by quarry workings.

❻ Later, swing **R** along wide grassy track climbing steeply through bracken to ridge, and go **L** for summit.

❼ Descend south on narrow footpath to reach fence above woods. Do not cross (as many have done), but follow fence down **L** to stile. After crossing stile go **R**, along path that leads back to lane near car park.

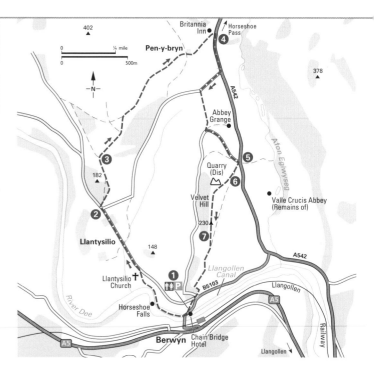

VALLE CRUCIS Idyllic Valle

From the Dee to the Eglwyseg, this walk discovers a fascinating tapestry of history and landscape.

6.75 miles/10.9km 4hrs **Ascent** 1,296ft/395m ⚠ **Difficulty** [2]

Paths Towpath, farm tracks and field paths, 5 stiles
Map OS Explorer 255 Llangollen and Berwyn **Grid ref** SJ 214420
Parking Long-stay car park in East Street, just south-west of the bridge

1 Walk from car park to main street and go **L** over Llangollen Bridge. Turn **R** then **L**, climbing to canal and dropping on to towpath by café.

2 After about 1 mile (1.6km) canal veers **L**. Leave towpath to cross canal on ivy-clad bridge. Turn **R** along pavement of main road (A542). Cross road and take farm track signed 'FP to Valle Crucis'. Track heads north past old abbey, where track ends. Footpath continues, along **L** field edge.

3 After crossing stile at Abbey Cottage turn **R** for few paces, then **L** to follow well-defined track through woodland. When you get to Hendre farm take **R-H** fork leading to narrow lane at Tan-y-Fron.

4 Turn **R** along road, heading towards prominent cliffs of Eglwyseg, then **R** again, along lane that hugs foot of cliffs.

5 After 0.25 mile (400m), leave through 2nd of adjacent gates on **R**. Walk away beside successive fields, crossing stile by farm sheds on to track back through to lane. Go **R** past junction.

6 When you reach 2nd junction take **R-H** fork for few paces, then go through gate on **R**, on to waymarked footpath leading to Castell Dinas Bran. From crumbling west walls of castle descend on zig-zag path. Go around **R-H** side of little knoll at bottom of hill to join track near house called Tirionfa.

7 At junction, keep ahead to 2nd cottage, there crossing stile into field. Trace **L-H** field edge down to narrow lane.

8 Across this, route continues along contained path, passing school before crossing road and then Llangollen Canal close to start of walk. Descend road down to Llangollen Bridge before crossing back into car park.

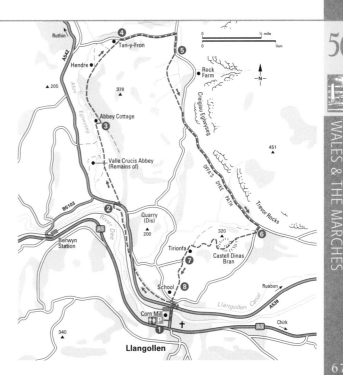

PRESTATYN Mountains Meet Sea

A nature walk through wooded hillsides and limestone knolls and a coastal panorama from Prestatyn to Llandudno's Great Orme.

3.5 miles/5.6km 2hrs **Ascent** 820ft/250m ⚠ **Difficulty** ⊡1⊡
Paths Well-defined woodland paths and tracks **Map** OS Explorer 264 Vale of Clwyd or 265 Clwydian Range **Grid ref** SJ 071821 **Parking** Picnic site at foot of hill

❶ Turn **R**, out of car park and climb few paces up steep lane. Turn **R** along public footpath marked with Offa's Dyke National Trail acorn sign. This enters area of scrubby woodland with wire fence to **R**, before climbing above quarry workings. As footpath reaches high fields, ignore all paths off to **L**.

❷ Continue along top edge of woods towards Tan-yr-Allt, eventually dropping to junction. Go **L**, passing above another quarry and then around wooded cove. Ignore path off **L** there, and later, at waymark, keep ahead towards Bryniau.

❸ Go through kissing gate on to metalled lane by Red Roofs. Turn **L** at next junction, then **R** few paces further on, to follow lane rounding south side of Graig Fawr.

❹ Turn **R** through gate on to Graig Fawr Estate and follow footpath leading to trig point on summit.

❺ Descend eastwards along grassy path that weaves through bracken to pass beneath overhead power cable at edge of wood. Now stepped, onward way drops beside fence into trees, emerging through kissing gate at bottom.

❻ Turn **R** along disused railway track, before taking 2nd footpath on **R**, that crosses field back towards Prestatyn Hillside. Turn **L** and follow footpath into Coed yr Esgob, woods at foot of Prestatyn Hillside.

❼ Where path divides, take upper fork that joins Bishopwood Lane. Follow this back to junction near car park at start of walk.

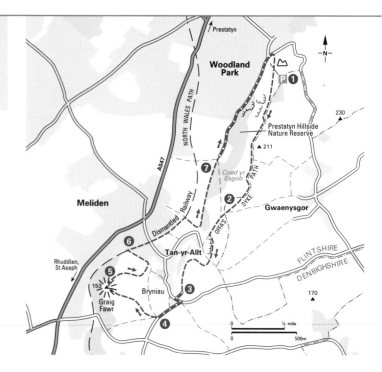

MOEL FAMAU The Mother Mountain

Walk to the highest of the Clwydian Hills.

8 miles/12.9km 4hrs 30min **Ascent** 1,608ft/490m ▲ **Difficulty** ③
Paths Well-defined paths and forestry tracks, 8 stiles **Map** OS Explorer 265 Clwydian Range
Grid ref SJ 198625 **Parking** Pay car park by Loggerheads Country Park Visitor Centre
NOTE Route can be shortened by taking regular Moel Famau shuttle bus, which runs on Sundays
(July to September) and bank holidays, from forestry car park to Loggerheads

❶ Pass front of Country Park Information Centre, café and other buildings, cross bridge over Alun and turn **L** along surfaced path through valley. Keep to main, near-level path, marked Leete Path.

❷ Pass the A.L.Y.N. Kennels, cross lane, then look out for small, often slippery path on **L** (signed 'Moel Famau'). This leads to footbridge. Across this, path heads west, then staggers to **R** across farm lane and climbs past farmhouse. Enclosed by thickets, it climbs **R** of another house to reach T-junction of country lanes. Go straight ahead and follow lane uphill, then turn **R** to follow track that passes Ffrith farm before swinging **L** to climb round pastured slopes of Ffrith Mountain. Take **L** fork in tracks (at grid ref 177637).

❸ Route skirts spruce plantation and climbs to crossroads of tracks, marked by tall waymarker post. Turn **L** here on wide path over undulating heather slopes towards tower on top of Moel Famau.

❹ From summit, head southeast and go through gate at end of wall to follow wide track, marked with red-tipped waymarker posts, southeast along forest's edge. Track continues its descent through trees to meet roadside car park/picnic area 0.75 mile (1.2km) east of Bwlch Penbarra's summit.

❺ Turn **L** along road, before turning **R** when you get to 1st junction. Quiet lane leads to busy A494. Cross main road with care and continue along hedge-lined lane staggered to **R**.

❻ Waymarked path on **L** heads northeast across fields towards banks of Alun. Don't cross river at bridge, but head north, through gateway and across fields, passing stone-built house below on **R**. Turn **R** on A494. It's just 0.5 mile (800m) from here to Country Park entrance, walk on verges and paths.

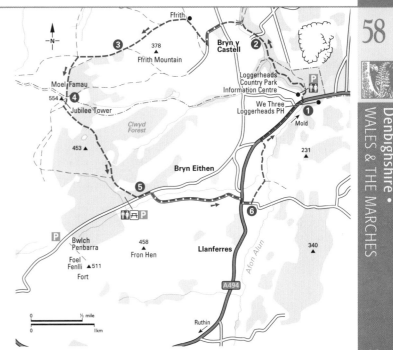

CEIRIOG VALLEY In The Beautiful Valley

Discover an earthly heaven in one of ancient Clwyd's truly green and pleasant valleys.

3.75 miles/6km 2hrs 30min **Ascent** 853ft/260m ⚠ **Difficulty** ①

Paths Sketchy paths and farm tracks, 4 stiles
Map OS Explorer 255 Llangollen & Berwyn **Grid ref** SJ 157328
Parking Roadside parking in village

❶ From The Hand, take eastbound lane past church and uphill with conifer plantation on **R** and pastures of Ceiriog below **L**.

❷ At far end of plantation leave road for farm track on **L**. This ends at barn. Keep **R** of barn and aim for gate beyond. Through gate maintain direction, over shoulder of grassy knoll, then aim for stile in fence ahead. Beyond this, cross another field down to gate, through which mount stile on **R**.

❸ Bear **L**, crossing 2 streamlets to join track past Ty'n-y-fedw farm. Don't go through gate, but follow grass path **R** beside fence, shortly entering wood.

❹ Keep ahead to far end of woods. Emerging into field, grass trod curves round to gate at top corner. Turn **R** along rising farm track, ignoring junctions to reach lane. Next cross to ongoing track opposite, which climbs on through high pastures.

❺ At crossroads, turn **R** along green track – part of Upper Ceiriog Way. This heads southwest towards green hill known as Cefn-Hîr-fynydd

❻ After about 300yds (274m) leave track through gate on **R**. If you head west by **R** edge of rushy area and towards Pen y Glôg's sparse crags, it will be easy to find small stile in next fence, then wooden gate on **L** soon afterwards. Through gate head downhill with faint sheep path past low clump of rocks on **L**, and aiming for distant farm of Cyrchynan-isaf.

❼ Lower down, developing grassy track runs on through valley of Nant y Glôg contouring lower slopes of Pen y Glôg, eventually reaching gate.

❽ After swinging **R** with lively stream track terminates by lane to south of Llanarmon Dyffryn Ceiriog. Follow lane past attractive cottages and village school to arrive by Hand Hotel in village square.

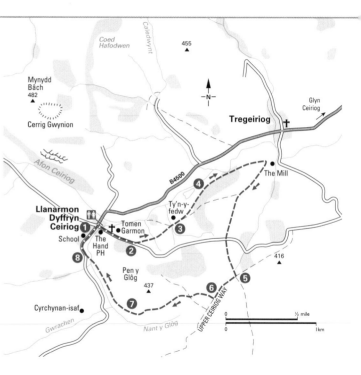

GREENFIELD VALLEY Grey Valley

Following monks, martyrs and merchants.

5 miles/8km 3hrs **Ascent** 558ft/170m ⚠ **Difficulty** [1]
Paths Woodland paths and tracks, lanes, field paths and coastal embankment, 9 stiles
Map OS Explorer 265 Clwydian Range **Grid ref** SJ 197775
Parking Just off A548 at Greenfield

❶ Take footpath that emerges from back of car park on **L-H** side and follow it around abbey.
❷ Turn **L** between visitor centre and old schoolhouse on track that passes Abbey Farm. Take **L** fork by brick walls of Abbey Wire Mill, following sign to Fishing Pool.
❸ Beyond Victoria Mill take lower **R-H** fork; bear **R** past fixed iron gates to pass crumbling remains of Meadow Mill. Beyond mill turn **L** up steps, climbing up by weir and back on to main track.
❹ Turn **R** along lower track, eventually passing above Hall's soft drinks factory. Beyond brick chimney, fork off **R** down to kissing gate and wind out to road. Turn **L** along road as far as St Winefride's Chapel and Well. Go back down road to Royal Oak Inn.
❺ Climb lane, called Green Bank, that begins from opposite side of road. Beyond houses bear off **R** along waymarked track. Keep ahead past entrance to small housing estate on sunken hedged path. Enter field over stile at top.

❻ Head out to distant **R** corner and continue at edge of next field. Maintain your northwesterly direction to stile and keep going to another, part-way down boundary. Walk on with hedge on your **R**, exiting over stile onto track.
❼ Leave cart track where it swings round to **R** for 2nd time and follow signed footpath across meadow and then through trees to banks of Afon Marsiandwr. After crossing stream path climbs out of woods and crosses field to country lane.
❽ Turn **R** along lane following it down to coast road (A548). Cross busy road with care. Continuing footpath to seashore lies immediately opposite you, over step stile. Cross field and then railway track, again with care as trains are not infrequent, and continue walking until you get to inner flood embankments where you turn **R**.
❾ Footpath comes out by Greenfield Dock. Turn **R** along lane into Greenfield. Turn **L** to return to car park.

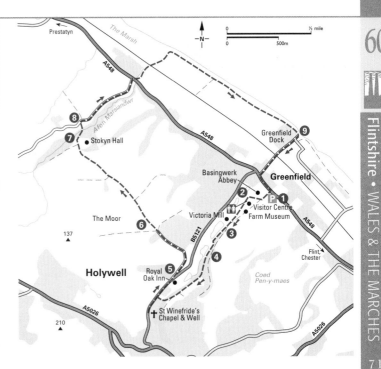

ASHPERTON Hereford's Lost Canal
Along an old waterway, now being restored.

7.75 miles/12.5km 3hrs 30min **Ascent** 260ft/79m ⚠ **Difficulty** 1
Paths Field and woodland paths, minor roads, at least 35 stiles
Map OS Explorer 202 Leominster & Bromyard **Grid ref** SO 642415
Parking St Bartholomew's Church, Ashperton

❶ From car park take 'forty shillings' gate, behind houses, following waymarkers. Join track to A417. Turn **L**, then **R**, beside high fence. Follow fingerpost across meadows for 600yds (549m). Find gate beside cricket net. Cross cricket field to sightscreen, then track, not joining Haywood Lane (to which track leads) until some 250yds (229m) further, at far corner. Turn **L**, passing Tunnel House. After 1 mile (1.6km) find stile on **L** beyond gate 100yds (91m) after Upleadon Court drive.
❷ Cross fields and ditch, then Upleadon Farm's driveway. Aim for far **L-H** corner, taking 3 gates, then skirt woodland to **L**, striking **L** (waymarked) at its corner, up field. At Gold Hill Farm go **R** of shed. Behind this, turn **L**, over 2 stiles. Turn **R**, ascending beside fence. From 1st corner follow hawthorn boundary remnant to road.
❸ Turn **L** for 0.25 mile (400m). Where road turns **L** go ahead, initially beside wood, entering field. Veer slightly **L** to find (hidden) handrailed bridge with broken stile beyond. Turn **L** but in 25yds (23m) turn **R**, before gate.

After 500yds (457m) enter trees. On leaving them strike half **R** for large White House.
❹ Turn **R** along road. At junction, take footpath opposite, across field. Beyond trees, aim **R** of solitary oak. Walk across fields, over 3 footbridges and under power lines, passing through gap in another stile, but do not cross this – note 3 waymarkers on far side. Turn **L**. Just beyond Homend find stile in far **L-H** corner of old orchard, shielded by ash and larch. Turn **L**, soon moving **R** to double gates flanking wide concrete bridge. After leafy avenue keep ahead, veering **R** when pond is behind trees to **L**. Cross driveway to Canon Frome Court, then track, finally reaching road by spinney.
❺ Cross and head to canal. Turn **L**. In 140yds (128m) turn **R**, over canal. Veer **L** and uphill, finding large oak in top **L-H** corner. Keep this line despite field boundary shortly curving away. At copse turn **R**, later moving **L** into indistinct lane. Village hall heralds A417. Turn **L** along pavement. Turn **R** to church and start.

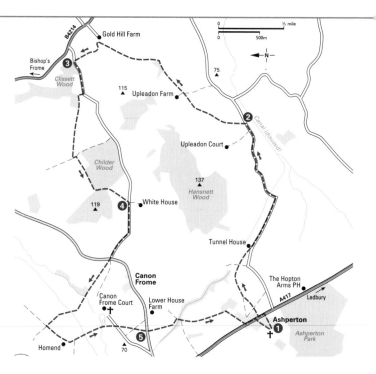

FROME VALLEY Two Churches

Discover secluded churches and special wild service trees amid pastures on this easy ramble.

4.75 miles/7.7km 2hrs 30min **Ascent** 475ft/145m ⚠ **Difficulty** [1]

Paths Field paths, dirt tracks, lanes and minor roads, 14 stiles

Map Explorer 202 Leominster & Bromyard **Grid ref** SO 680502

Parking Roadside just before grassy lane to Acton Beauchamp's church– please tuck in tightly

❶ Leave churchyard by iron gate in top corner. Ascend to stile. Turn **L**, walking inside orchard edge. Leave by stile at 1st corner. Contour next field to stile then descend slightly to another, hidden stile 100yds (91m) **R** of solitary tree. Turn **R**, through gate here, ascending by field edge. Keep this line, but, on seeing gate with blue waymarker at protruding corner of Halletshill Coppice, drop straight down, finding steps to footbridge.

❷ Now go straight up bank. After trees, keep hedge on **R** to a minor road. Turn **R** (and visit church). Return to road and turn **R**. At entrance to The Hawkins take kissing gate, then follow waymarkers across track to skirt farm. Now head down pastures to stile with wooden steps. Keep ahead, descending gently, for 200yds (183m), to cross footbridge over Linton Brook.

❸ Turn **L**, walking beside brook for 0.6 mile (1km), to road. Turn **L** for 160yds (146m). Turn **R**. Now driveway to Upper Venn Farm runs for 0.5 mile (800m). Just before 1st shed turn **L** to gate 50yds (46m) along field edge.

❹ Cross field diagonally, to gate in **L** hedge. Turn **L** across field, aiming slightly uphill, beside residual mature oaks to stile beyond electricity pole. Pick up rough track to Venn Farm, passing alongside its black barn. Admire farm's cream walls and exposed timbers, then turn away, along drive. Follow this down to minor road.

❺ Turn **L**, passing Paunton Court (home to Frome Valley Vineyard) on sharp bend. At crossroads go straight over. Climbing this quite steep lane, Church of St Giles comes into view. Take 1st **L** turning to return to car.

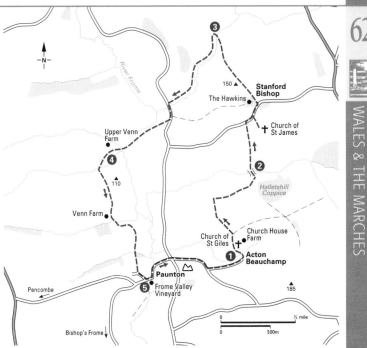

HEREFORD CITY Historic Streets
Around a charming medieval city.

2.75 miles/4.4km 1hr 30min **Ascent** Negligible ⚠ **Difficulty** 1
Paths City streets, riverside path and tracks **Map** OS Explorer 189 Hereford & Ross-on-Wye
Grid ref SO 510403 **Parking** Garrick House long-stay, pay-and-display multi-storey car park,
Widemarsh Street **NOTE** Several busy junctions without subways – care needed

❶ Turn **L** out of car park. After 150yds (137m) is Coningsby Hospital now Coningsby Museum. Go back short way to walk along Coningsby Street, to T-junction. Turn **R** on Monkmoor Street. Turn **R** into Commercial Road. At the Blueschool Street junction is city wall, while on near side are magistrates' courts.
❷ Cross Commercial Road then Bath Street. Follow Union Street. Go **R** to High Town. Go **L** down Church Street, to Hereford Cathedral (tourist information centre on **R**).
❸ Go **L**, beside cathedral, passing stonemasons' workshop. Go along Castle Street. Shortly before Castle House (hotel) turn **R** to Castle Green. Hug railings on **L**, beside Castle Pool (part of original moat), to walk above the green and Nelson Column (1809). Zig-zag down to cross Victoria Bridge.
❹ Turn **R** (or **L** for extended riverside stroll), passing putting green, tennis courts and flood defences completed in 2008. Keeping on south side of river,

cross St Martin's Street to go under Greyfriars Bridge, continuing to Hunderton Bridge.
❺ Cross this old railway bridge. Take steps down to head back towards city. Skirt rowing club, then walk up Greyfriars Avenue. Before junction go half **R** across car park to go through pedestrian subway. (But go **R**, through car subway, to see large chunk of city wall.) Brick building in front of you is built on city wall. Up hallow steps, cross St Nicholas' Street with care.
❻ As you begin along Victoria Street, see solitary tree. Few paces beyond it, about 10ft (3m) up in city wall, is a hemispherical hollow, supposedly made by cannon ball embedded during siege of Hereford in 1645. (Cannon ball is in museum above library.) Go along West Street to Broad Street. Turn **L**. Walk towards All Saints Church. Turn **R** then shortly **L**, down Widemarsh Street, to return to car.

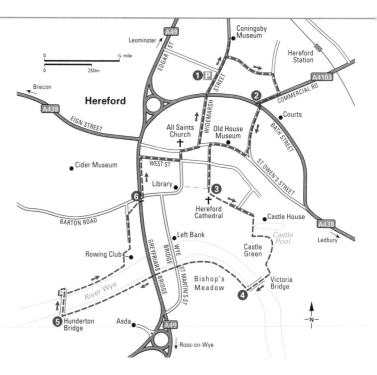

COPPET HILL Beside The River Wye

A peaceful walk with fine views.

6.75 miles/10.9km 2hrs 45min **Ascent** 855ft/260m ⚠ **Difficulty** ②

Paths Quiet lanes, riverside meadows, woodland paths, 2 stiles
Map OS Explorer OL14 Wye Valley & Forest of Dean **Grid ref** SO 575196
Parking Goodrich Castle pay-and-display car park open daily, times vary with the season

① Walk to castle access road junction; turn quickly **L**. In 110yds (100m) cross bridge over B4229.

② Go up further 400yds (366m). Ignore road branching off **R**, but enjoy view of Kerne Bridge. Opposite, between 2 roads, sign 'Coppet Hill Common' indicates return route.

③ Go 0.5 mile (800m) up this dead end, to cattle grid. At brow, woods give way to parkland. Go ahead for 325yds (297m) to horse chestnut tree at **R** turn.

④ Keep ahead for another 400yds (366m), bending **L** and dipping down, road once again tree-lined. Road curves slightly **R**, while gravel track goes up ramp and fractionally **L**.

⑤ Curve **R**. Ignore pillared driveway but begin down youth hostel's driveway. At welcome sign take footpath that runs initially parallel to it. Descend steps and sometimes muddy path to T-junction beside River Wye.

⑥ Turn **R**, following Wye Valley Walk (turn **L** to visit church). In 350yds (320m) reach old, iron girder railway bridge, which now carries Wye Valley Walk across river, but stay this side, passing under bridge. In about 160yds (146m) look carefully for yellow bands of 'rights of way' tape on tree.

⑦ Take path closest to river. Continue for 1.25miles (2km). Enter Coldwell Wood to walk beside river for further 0.25 mile (400m). On leaving, keep by river in preference to path that follows woodland's edge. In 350yds (320m) reach stile beside fallen willow.

⑧ Turn **R**, signposted 'Coppet Hill', passing through line of trees to stile. Soon begin arduous woodland ascent. Path levels, later rising to The Folly, then goes down (not up!) to triangulation point. Follow clear green sward ahead, becoming narrow rut then stepped path, down to road, close to Point **③**. Retrace steps to castle car park.

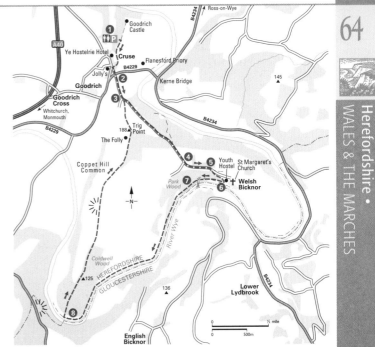

AYMESTREY Rocks Of Ages

Around a redeveloped quarry now used for grazing and woodland.

4.75 miles/7.7km 2hrs 30min **Ascent** 525ft/160m **⚠ Difficulty** 1

Paths Excellent tracks, field paths, minor roads, steep woodland sections, 11 stiles

Map OS Explorer 203 Ludlow **Grid ref** SO 426658

Parking At old quarry entrance, on east side of A4110, 0.25 mile (400m) north of Aymestrey Bridge

❶ Walk up access road for 750yds (686m), until just before junction of tracks. Note stile on **R** – route returns over this.

❷ Turn **L** then, in 25yds (23m), curve **R**, passing house with stone wall relic in its garden. Shortly curve **L**. Walk through Yatton, to T-junction. Turn **L** to A4110. Cross to stile, striking across this field to gap. In next field veer **L** to skirt **R** edge of (not over) embankment, to find corner stile. Walk up **L** field edge but, at brow, where it bends for 70yds (64m) to corner, take stile in hedge to walk along other side. Within 60yds (55m) you are on clear path, down through woodland, ravine on **L**. Join rough driveway to minor road.

❸ Turn **L** here, joining Mortimer Trail. Enjoy this wooded, riverside lane for nearly 0.75 mile (1.2km), to A4110 again. Cross, then walk for 25yds (23m) to **R**. Take raised green track, heading for hills. Then go diagonally across 2 fields, to stile and wooden steps.

❹ Within few paces fork **L** to ascend steeply through trees. Leave by stile, to cross 2 meadows diagonally. Over double stile, walk along **L-H** field edge, still heading downhill. At trees turn **L**. Soon reach tarmac road. Turn **L** along road, now going back uphill. Beyond Hill Farm, enter Croft Estate. Walk along this hard gravel track. After 110yds (100m), ignore **R** fork but, 550yds (503m) further on, you must leave it. This spot is identified where deciduous trees give way to conifers on **L** and you see Mortimer Trail marker post on wide ride between larches and evergreens on **R**.

❺ Turn **L** (no signpost). Within 110yds (100m) go half **R** and more steeply down on aged access track. Within 250yds (229m) look out for modern wooden gate, waymarked, leading out of woods. Walk along **R-H** edge, admiring former quarry's new landscape. Walk briefly in trees then out and, at far corner, within field, turn **L** to Point ❷. Retrace steps to start of walk.

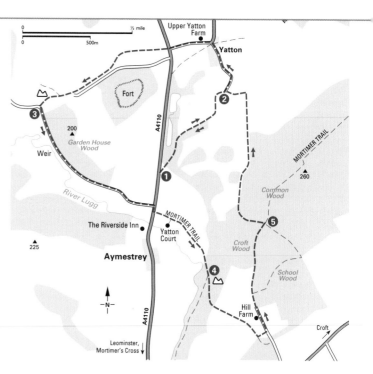

DOWNTON ON THE ROCK Picturesque Castle

A landscape designed to please the eye.

10 miles/16.1km 5hrs **Ascent** 1,200ft/366m ⚠ **Difficulty** ③

Paths Pastures, leafy paths, grass or dirt tracks, tarmac lanes, steep bank, 13 stiles
Map OS Explorer 203 Ludlow **Grid ref** SO 403741
Parking Community centre and village hall car park, Leintwardine

❶ Begin downhill, soon taking 1st **L**, Church Street. Turn **L**. At school, turn **R**. Aim for brown-and-white house but, after 2-plank footbridge, go **L** to tarmac road. Turn **R**. In 300yds (274m) turn **L**, to A4113. Cross, turn **R** up lane. Ascend for 1 mile (1.6km). Soon after skew junction go forward, taking **L** of 2 gates. Just beyond corrugated shelter, take stile on **R**. Go three-quarters **L**, across 2 fields, to woodland. At A4113 turn **L** but soon **R**, beside wire fence. At end follow field edge **L** for 40yds (37m). Go down earthy bank in trees to pass stables on **R**, then along dirt road, soon straight to Brakes Farm.
❷ Go ahead (waymarker). Cross minor road diagonally, then cross fields to minor lane beside houses Nos 20 and 19. Turn **L**. Soon turn **R**, downhill. Turn **R**, along river, just before bridge over River Teme. Skirt 2 unnamed houses. Up bank, join dirt road. Follow this to Castle Bridge. Ascend but within 110yds (100m) of leaving woodland go half **R**, across field, rejoining dirt road into forest for 60yds (55m). (If footpath is not established, go round road, avoiding crop.) Scramble

up bank (waymarker). Traverse steep meadow to gate in top, among oaks. Keep this line to go down meadow, locating stile on **L** into harvested trees.
❸ Turn **L** and descend. At meadow, curve round dry valley. At **L** bend go through gate on **R**. Go **L** of specimen oak to hidden stile in bottom corner. Cross footbridge and turn **R**. Cross meadow to gate, and soon reach minor road. Turn **R**. Descend easily through Burrington, to St George's Church. Behind church, cross meadows to Burrington Bridge. Cross River Teme. After 650yds (594m) take **R** turn. In Downton, head towards Old Downton Lodge, but then turn **L**. Beyond wall take the **R** gate (waymarker), along old lane. Shortly move **R** to ascend **R-H** field edge, soon following beech-lined avenue to reach junction with dirt track.
❹ Over stile into field, swing **L** to descend. Past small (possibly dry) pond veer **L** along **R-H** field edge to road. Turn **R**. Within 275yds (251m), at Wisteria Cottage, take kissing gate. Cross 3 fields to soon emerge on Watling Street. Turn **R** to Church Street and back to start.

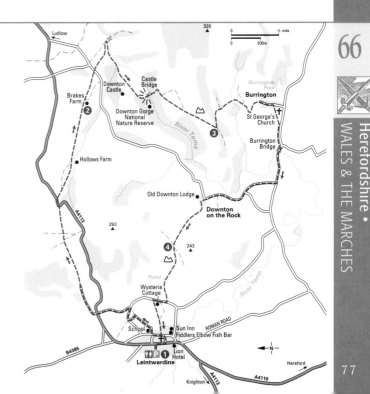

KILPECK Orcop Hill

A walk once enjoyed by Violette Szabo, a wartime heroine.

4.75 miles/7.7km 2hrs 15min **Ascent** 590ft/180m ⚠ **Difficulty** 2

Paths Field paths, tracks and minor lanes, 21 stiles

Map OS Explorer 189 Hereford & Ross-on-Wye **Grid ref** SO 445304

Parking Spaces beside St Mary's and St David's Church, Kilpeck

① Walk down to Red Lion, turn **R** and at junction, follow 'Garway Hill'. Take 2nd fingerpost to hug hedge just behind The Knoll (house). Move **R**, to stand beside stile from The Knoll's garden. Aim for **L** side of white house 3 fields away. Cross on to this lane, immediately turn **L** and follow waymarkers through trees. Go straight down field to near junction.

② Turn **L**, past Two Brooks. After 500yds (457m) turn **L**, through gate by Grafton Oak, tucked behind. Soon in scenic meadow, follow fence until crossing stile. Now keep ahead but drift down, guided by gigantic oak. Stile you need is ahead, not another, further down, that crosses brook. Contour with trees on **L** for 2 fields. In 3rd find footbridge down and **L**.

③ Follow waymarkers, diagonally up field. Walk with wire fence on **R**. Leave this long field at its top end (but, oddly, waymarked route seems intrusive, crossing and re-crossing wire fence on **R** near Greenways, via wooded area). Go up (leftish) to opening beside hollow oak. Move **L** to walk along **L-H** field edge. Ignore waymarker into **L-H** field –way out has disappeared. Instead keep straight, to tarmac road. Turn **L**. After 650yds (594m) fingerpost slants **L**.

④ Take path through bracken to track. Turn **R** for 25yds (23m), then **L**, to pass **R** of Saddlebow Farm. Avenue below leads into field. Walk along this **R** edge, to just before another gate. Join good track, following it for 650yds (594m), to 3 gates in corner.

⑤ Take 2nd on **L**. Beyond New House Farm go 0.25 mile (400m) to junction. Don't turn down to Kilpeck yet! Go 160yds (146m) further. Go **L** just beyond Size Croft Barns. Descend to unseen gap 120yds (110m) **R** of bottom **L-H** corner. Out of copse, cross 2 fields to pass between buildings of The Priory. Avenue of horse chestnuts leads to Red Lion.

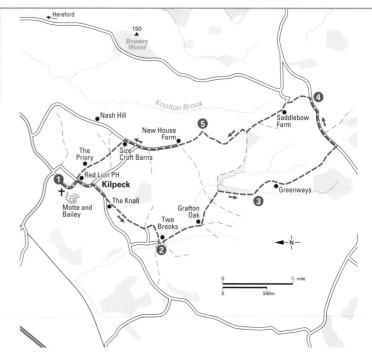

ABBEY DORE Golden Valley

In search of a 19th-century workhouse.

8 miles/12.9km 3hrs 45min **Ascent** 540ft/165m ⚠ **Difficulty** 2
Paths Meadows, tracks and woodland paths (one awkward descent), 22 stiles
Map OS Explorer OL13 Brecon Beacons (East) **Grid ref** SO 386302
Parking East side of B4347 facing south

❶ Cross B4347 at lychgate. Slant to field's top **L** corner. Go through gap near white cottage's garden, hugging hedge on **L** to stile. In 20yds (18m), turn **R** up hedged lane to Ewyas Harold Common.

❷ This is prescribed route but many paths and tracks criss-cross here. Across concrete track take **L** diagonal ride. In 65yds (60m) take slightly **L** option. After 45yds (41m) bear **R**. In 275yds (251m), beyond solitary tree, fork **R** for 40yds (37m). Trees behind, bracken in front, turn **L**, soon descending for 200yds (183m) to multiple junction. Go half **L** on grass. After 120yds (110m) turn **L** on gravel track. Just beyond seat, fork **R** down rutted track. After 3 houses swing **R**, over cattle grid.

❸ In village, turn **R** then **R** again. At sharp bend, ascend steps. Aim **L** of spinney. After old buildings ascend 3 fields. Waymarker takes you into trees alongside wire fence. Leave trees, swing up to boundary corner. Keep field edges **R**, passing ruin, to Plash Farm.

❹ Walk through farmyard; get behind farmhouse by turning **R** twice. Go to bottom corner. Sunken lane leads to road. Turn **R**, then **L** to Dulas Court. Cross brook by bridge beside new buildings. Turn **R** through orchard. Go diagonally up meadow into conifers. Walk uphill to track, turn **R** for another 40yds (37m), then fork **R**, uphill, following waymarkers. Out of woodland, aim for pole, then pass between buildings (Cot Farm).

❺ Keep hedge **L** across waymarked fields, to common. In 70yds (64m) join track (**L** part of hairpin), then 70yds (64m) further, go ahead on green sward, soon joining track. Some 50yds (46m) before house turn **L**. Waymarked stiles lead to lane by Cwm Farm. Turn **R**. Before Abbey Dore Court Garden find stile at bridge. In field with poplars at end, find gate part-way down on **R**.

❻ Waymarked stiles lead to Riverdale. Retrace your steps to Point **❻**. Now keep on east side of river. Turn **L** at road. In 60yds (55m), take waymarked route between military fence and gardens. Footbridge, meadow and agricultural graveyard lead to abbey.

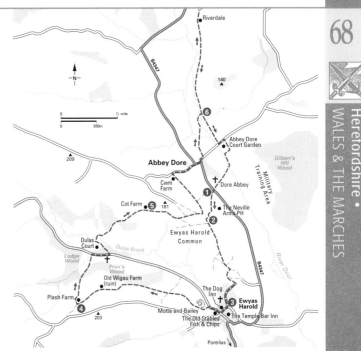

69

Herefordshire •
WALES & THE MARCHES

HERGEST RIDGE Overlooking Wales
Up to a glorious ridge overlooking Wales.

7.5 miles/12.1km 3hrs 30min **Ascent** 1,115ft/340m ▲ **Difficulty** ③
Paths Meadows, field paths, excellent tracks, 12 stiles **Map** OS Explorer 201 Knighton & Presteigne
Grid ref SO 295565 **Parking** Mill Street car park (east and west sides of Crabtree Street)

❶ Walk down High Street. Take alley on **R**, between hairdresser and menswear shop. Zig-zag to Bridge Street. Turn **R**. Cross River Arrow. Take driveway to Newburn Farm.

❷ Go round 3 sides, then take gate beyond corrugated shed and stables into field. After area planted with trees, when you see footbridge, move up and **L** to take stile to **R-H** field edge, under oak limbs. Walk for 0.5 mile (800m) through meadows, curving **L** to stile and steps, between 2 houses, down to road.

❸ Turn **R**, then **R** again to cross Hergest Bridge but after 125yds (114m) take **L** fingerpost. Within 100yds (91m) veer **R** to cross stile into trees. Out of trees, see stile ahead, but go beyond it to waymarker, to cross meadow to sweet chestnuts. Over difficult stile, turn **R**, along awkward path across steep, wooded bank. After 325yds (297m), stile puts you into another meadow. Cross footbridge. Contour to gate then cross waymarked meadows using 2-plank bridge, double-stiled footbridge and steps down to metal footbridge.

❹ At road on caravan site for seasonal farm workers turn **R**. After 40yds (37m) find stile (perhaps overgrown), **R**. Almost immediately, take 2nd stile beside huge, damaged oak. At track beside Mahollam Farm bear **R**, downhill. Don't stay on this lane, but go **R**, finding another footbridge. Ascend steeply, soon in farmland. Cross fields to lane. Turn **R**. Go **L** for 325yds (297m), to gate. Now go straight up to '423m' trig point on Hergest Ridge, avoiding densest gorse.

❺ Keep ahead for 80yds (73m) but, on seeing wide path cut through bracken, go quarter **R**; beyond it lies pool. Turn **R**. Now walk 1.5 miles (2.4km), ignoring early **L** fork. On road again, when 30yds (27m) beyond sign proclaiming 'Kington – the centre for walking', turn **R**. Round Haywood Farm, continue down to cattle grid; cross. Down this road after 350yds (320m), look for fingerpost beside white 'No. 31'. Go down field. Turn away from Kington for 120yds (110m); turn sharply **L**, following 'Tatty Moor'. Cross meadows to recreation ground. Join Park Avenue, which becomes Mill Street.

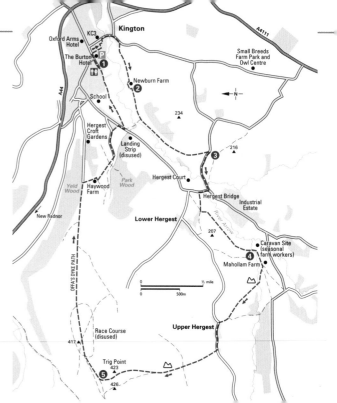

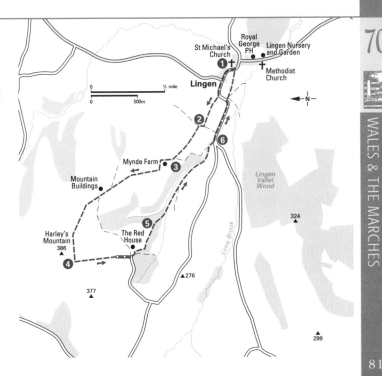

HARLEY'S MOUNTAIN Bracing Air

A brisk walk In farming country.

3.75 miles/6km 2hrs **Ascent** 755ft/230m ⚠ **Difficulty** 2
Paths Meadows, field paths, woodland tracks with roots, 11 stiles
Map OS Explorer 201 Knighton & Presteigne **Grid ref** SO 364672
Parking At St Michael's Church, Lingen (tuck in well)

1 Walk from church; cross to minor road signposted 'Willey'. At 1st bend, follow fingerpost ahead. Beyond difficult gate beside corrugated shed, walk by **R** edge of this paddock and next, reaching little-used lane in trees.
2 Move **R** to strike up field, passing oak stump. Follow waymarker up and slightly **R**. In corner, negotiate rusty gate between better ones. At brick-built cottage skirt **R** of this and collapsed buildings of Mynde Farm. Find gate **R** behind low building still standing.
3 Go down and up meadow to stile seen from afar. Veer **L**, passing beside Mountain Buildings on deeply rutted, rocky track. Some 160yds (146m) on, enter field. Go diagonally across field (but if ridged with crops, follow 2 field edges **L**); then keep that line, now with hedge **L**. Within 200yds (183m) take gate on **L**. 2 fields further along this breezy ridge reach another gate with small pool to **R** (possibly dry in high summer). Above and behind you is dull, grey trig point.
4 Turn **L** along sunken lane. Descend for 650yds (594m). At bottom move **L**, down to gate. Through

trees, shortly emerge close to The Red House. Go dead ahead, finding narrow path within trees, **R** of garage and beside hedge. Within 40yds (37m) negotiate metal gate. Do not be tempted down; instead move **L** (yellow waymarker, not blue), beside wire fence for few paces, then, maintaining fence's line, proceed to walk below narrow ridge on faint green tractor track for perhaps 100yds (91m). When ground ahead drops steeply into dell, turn half **L** to walk in trees beside meadow (field edge is easier). In 2nd meadow, where trees bulge out **L**, dive back into woodland – waymarker on oak (**R**).
5 Go steadily ahead, sometimes boggy, in woodland, lush pasture, then bracken for 0.5 mile (800m). At wobbly silver-grey gate drop **L** 10ft (3m) to waymarked stile into once pollarded, streamside lane. Reach road.
6 Turn **L**. After 450yds (411m), on bend, go straight down field to hedge beside farm buildings. Find single-plank stile in **L** corner. Go ahead, to stile that gives on to tvillage road – take care! Turn **L** to start (or go **R** and cross carefully, to go via church to your car).

BLACK HILL A Harsh Life

Visit the highest point in the two counties, where the harsh life was portrayed in Bruce Chatwin's 1938 book On the Black Hill.

8.75 miles/14.1km 4hrs **Ascent** 1,475ft/450m ⚠ **Difficulty** ③
Paths Muddy patches, stony descent, lanes, minor roads, 5 stiles **Map** OS Explorer OL13 Brecon Beacons (East) **Grid ref** SO 288328 **Parking** Black Hill car park (signposted)

❶ From car park cross stile to go straight and steeply up clear track. Enjoy airy path, or, if wind is strong, walk in lee on eastern side when terrain permits. Gradient varies over 1.5 miles (2.4km) to trig point.

❷ Fork **L**, leaving pond to **R**. Follow what is now easy, broad ridge for 1.75 miles (2.8km), to low, concrete slab. Turn **L**, on initially flagged path, joining both Offa's Dyke Path and border between England and Wales. In little over 0.5 mile (800m) is very indistinct top –over 2,300ft (700m).

❸ Now carry on for 2.5 miles (4km) along ridge: where you turn off is indicated by pile of stones and similar concrete slab indicating Offa's Dyke Path again – this point is approximately perpendicular to sharp end of Black Hill. You may be able to see your car from here.

❹ Turn **L**. Descent begins with **L-H** traverse. After 650yds (594m) be sure to swing round to **R**, heading down valley. When 140yds (128m) beyond this sharp bend, note, but do not take, waymarker indicating

L turn option (in late summer waymarker may be concealed by bracken). After 30yds (27m) come to finely forked junction.

❺ Be sure to take lower, **L-H** option; do not go 'straight on', that is, **R** fork. Descend to fence. Turn **R** in front of stile, cross stream and reach kissing gate within 50yds (46m). Some 160yds (146m) further is kissing gate by tree stump. Walk along sunken track, then go down old sunken lane. Later ignore stile on **L** and reach minor road.

❻ Turn **L** to descend to junction. Turn **L**. Within 60yds (55m) take footpath on **R**, down into trees to cross Olchon Brook, then re-ascend. Go round buildings at Blackhill Farm and continue up following waymarkers through trees to road you came in on. Turn **L**, then **R** to return to your car.

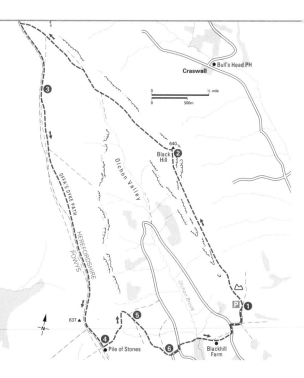

CLIFFORD Original Settlement

A 'backwater' of the River Wye.

5.5 miles/8.8km 2hrs 30min **Ascent** 560ft/171m ⚠ **Difficulty** 1

Paths Field paths and lanes, awkward embankment, over 30 stiles
Map OS Explorer 201 Knighton & Presteigne **Grid ref** SO 251450
Parking Roadside parking at St Mary's Church, near Clifford

❶ Just past road junction at corner of churchyard, take steps on **R**. Yellow arrows indicate route. On leaving Ton Wood arrows lead across old railway towards Clifford. Leave last meadow beside house, noting 2 arrows for those coming from Clifford.

❷ Walk to road. Turn **L** then **R** for castle. Retrace steps to Point ❷. Now take arrow pointing to oaks. At tarmac beyond follow 'Unsuitable for heavy goods vehicles'. On **R**, after 440yds (402m) search for stile up 3 steps. It's probably hidden by hazel. Across this green strip scramble down, then use steps to get up railway embankment again. Half-way up field switch hedge from **L** to your **R**. Find smart metal gate beside derelict yellow harvester. Wooded path soon reaches lane.

❸ Turn **L**. In 230yds (210m), before a stone dwelling, strike **R**, to stile behind 6 hawthorns in dip. Alongside garden, take rough track joining 2 tarmac lanes. Turn **R** for perhaps 30 paces. Waymarker points towards stile in trees. Go straight down field to meet lane.

❹ Turn **L** along lane for 0.5 mile (800m) to B4352.

Turn **R**. In 120yds (110m), cross to stile. In this vast meadow aim **R** of trees on skyline, then stile by white-walled house.

❺ Pass through garden. Take bridleway, **R**. Eventually join stony track, soon straight, but within 160yds (146m), where footpath crosses, turn **R**. To reach Holy Trinity Church go forward over stiles to driveway and turn **R**.

❻ Return to Point ❺. Go diagonally **L** to stile completely hidden by protruding hedge. Turn **R**, around 2 sides of field. In the next one turn **R**, along field edge to B4352 at footbridge and stile. Cross to take fingerpost seen **R**. Cross 2 fields; in 3rd keep ahead at corner but veer 1 small field **L** to gate (not road gate). Aim well **R** of oak to jutting out corner. Over stile here, aim for gap behind nearer solitary tree. Walk to seen road. Recross this field diagonally to gap, guided by other finger on post. Veer **L** to stile. Turn **R** beside woodland. Soon turn **R** by finding double stile in hedgerow to contour above Priory Farm. Having skirted **R** of house, St Mary's Church, across fields, is easily reached.

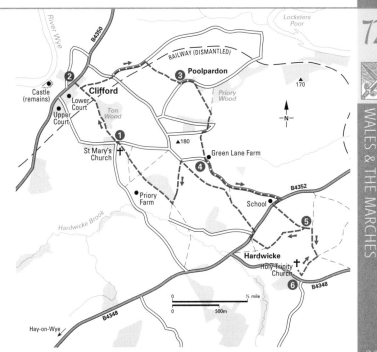

CLEEVE HILL A Fruity Route
Walking in Victoria plum country.

4.5 miles/7.2km 2hrs **Ascent** 225ft/69m ⚠ **Difficulty** 1

Paths Paths across fields, stony tracks and village roads, 5 stiles

Map OS Explorer 205 Stratford-upon-Avon & Evesham **Grid ref** SP 077469 **Parking** Outside Littleton Village Hall on School Lane, Middle Littleton, or village street (tithe barn parking for visitors only)

❶ Walk westwards up School Lane to B4085 (Cleeve Road). Cross diagonally **L** to take rutted, stony track. At junction of tracks turn **R** to pass beside gate, then another, following blue arrow. After 350yds (320m), reach opening on **R** and plum trees making field boundary; on **L** is metal gate.

❷ Through this gate enter Worcestershire Wildlife Trust's Windmill Hill Nature Reserve. Descend, ignoring crossing tracks, to stile and across 1 field to B4510. Follow signposted 'Cleeve Prior' footpath through Offenham Park caravan site. Take stile out of caravan park to walk on stone track beside river.

❸ At log cabin move to **R** to take double-stiled footbridge and resume your riverside stroll. Continue through mostly ungated pastures for over 0.75 mile (1.2km). Through small gate, leave river by taking **R-H** fork. Ascend through trees to clearing and path junction.

❹ Turn sharply **R** back on yourself, soon walking into trees again, to follow popular (and sometimes muddy) bridleway. In shade under 1 mile (1.6km) B4510 cuts through hill, beside The Hills. Cross and move **R** to fingerpost, but follow path for just 75yds (69m).

❺ Go through gate into nature reserve here, and follow waymarked, contouring path, giving fine views west. After 440yds (402m) recognise outward route. Turn **L** here, up bank, retracing steps for just 30yds (27m), to Point ❷. Once at top go straight across, walking with line of plum trees on **L-H** side. When this ends, maintain direction until you reach B4085.

❻ Cross road and go straight ahead. From 2nd field you will see tithe barn. Before young trees take kissing gate to **R**. In 15yds (14m) turn **L** to visit tithe barn, or keep ahead to village road. Turn **R** again, shortly to reach your car.

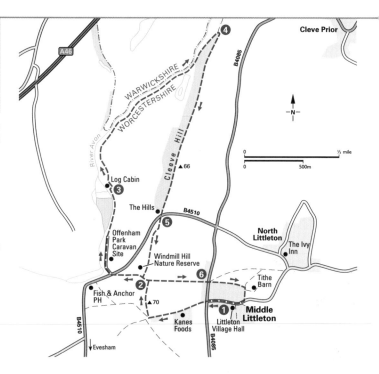

TARDEBIGGE The Ups And Downs
Visit Worcestershire's famous big wet steps

5.5 miles/8.8km 2hrs 30min **Ascent** 295ft/90m ⚠ **Difficulty** 2

Paths Towpath, pastures, field paths and minor lanes, 14 stiles
Map OS Explorer 204 Worcester & Droitwich Spa **Grid ref** SO 974682
Parking Limited space, so park tightly and considerately, on north and east side of road bridge

❶ Cross bridge No. 51 and turn **L**, taking towpath on south side of canal. Follow this to point about 15yds (14m) before next bridge – No. 52.

❷ Turn **R** into trees, then down field. Cross double-stiled footbridge among trees then keep ahead, over driveway to Patchetts Farm. At 3-way fingerpost keep ahead (4th finger missing!) to skirt copse to **L**, then stile and 2-plank bridge. Cross 2 fields, keeping hedge on **L**. Reach gate on **L**, close to broken oak tree.

❸ Turn **R**. Within 110yds (100m), go through gate ahead (no waymarker), ignoring 1 **L**. Go quarter **R** (or skirt crops) to stile in wire fence. Retain diagonal to cross simple footbridge of 3 planks, then find stile in next field's corner. Walk with hedge on **L** to reach minor road junction. Turn **R** for about 55yds (50m). Turn **L** to cross undulating pasture, passing pond to **L** and swapping field edge sides at new metal gate, to reach minor road.

❹ Turn **R**. Follow this for 0.5 mile (800m), taking 'Woodgate' at junction, to Lower Bentley Farm's driveway. Go 140yds (128m) to fingerpost **R**. Cross pasture diagonally to gap, then to another **R** of white house. Find stile in bottom **R-H** corner of this next field. Go forward for 75yds (69m) then three-quarters **L** to road.

❺ Turn **R** and in 75yds (69m) take handrailed, 3-planked footbridge. Cross pastures (waymarked) towards Orchard Farm, but then turn **R**, away from it. Over corner stile go ahead. At double stile (across ditch) go half **L**, and at gap in hedge (perhaps with wooden bar) turn **R** for 75yds (69m) to 2 new metal kissing gates. Now turn **L**, initially with field edge on **R**, for 650yds (594m), aiming well **L** of black-and-white house. At double stile, for stile and gate. Soon reach road.

❻ Turn **R**. At T-junction turn **L**. Join canal towpath this side of Stoke Pound Bridge. Now you have over 0.75 mile (1.2km) to return to car at the road bridge, approximately mid-way up Tardebigge Flight.

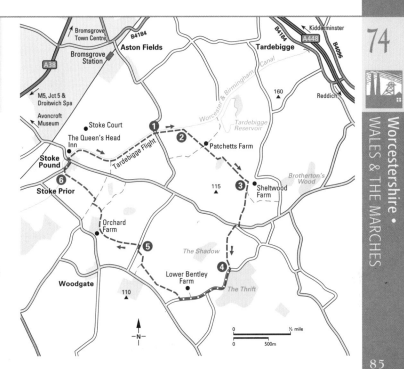

HANBURY HALL The Ice Houses

A stroll around an estate park.

4.75 miles/7.7km 2hrs 15min **Ascent** 250ft/76m ⚠ **Difficulty** 1

Paths Meadows, tracks and easy woodland paths, 12 stiles **Map** OS Explorer 204 Worcester & Droitwich Spa **Grid ref** SO 957652 **Parking** Piper's Hill car park, on B4091 between Stoke Works and Hanbury (fast road and no sign – easily missed!)

❶ From bottom of car park, follow driveway to Knotts Farm. Go ahead on **L-H** of 2 seemingly parallel paths. Keep ahead at post then, about 350yds (320m) after farm, reach gravel track at fingerpost.

❷ Go ahead, with field boundary on **L** ascending towards church, to stake with 2 waymarkers.

❸ Fork **L**, soon passing spinney, then losing height across meadow. Take care as stile and steps here spill you on to minor but fast road. Across this, go beside school. Cross 1 field directly then fraction **R**, walking diagonally in 3rd field, 30yds (27m) **R** of fenced oak, to metal gate. In 70yds (64m) cross footbridge on **L**. 2 stiles lead to Pumphouse Lane.

❹ Turn **R**. Take stile and gate on **R** just beyond black-and-white Grumbleground Cottage. In 40yds (37m), cross 3-plank footbridge. Follow electricity poles for 2 fields. Turn **R**, alongside wire fence. Reach road.

❺ Cross road to footpath opposite. At stile go half **L**, guided by wire fence. Pass close to Hanbury Hall's entrance, soon easing from perimeter wall to walk across parkland, striking minor road just beyond picturesque pond **R**. (Line of young trees will be to **L**.)

❻ Ignore minor road, turning immediately **R**. Hug boundary fence of coppice. Continue down **R-H** field edge. At junction turn R at National Trust sign, into this former deer park. After just 60yds (55m), at drainage ditch, edge **R** (blue National Trust arrow). Go straight, to stile to **L** of fenced trees, which hide pond. Maintain line up incline – look out for Hanbury church **L** – to tarmac driveway.

❼ Turn **L**. When it curves **R** go straight ahead to walk in oak avenue. Keep this line for 700yds (640m), to minor road. Turn **R**, then **L** up to church. Through churchyard, find kissing gate. Shortly rejoin outward route at Point ❸. Remember to go **L**, into woods, at Point ❷.

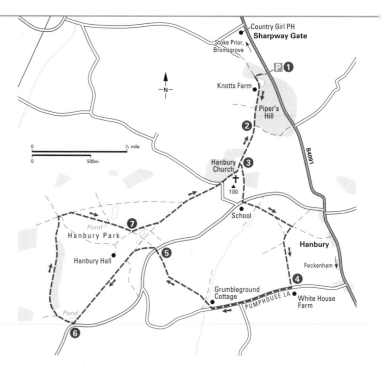

CLENT HILLS A Treat In Springtime

A brief circuit of the most visited hills in Worcestershire and where, in spring, fields of oilseed rape flood the landscape with colour.

3.5miles/5.7km 2hrs **Ascent** 660ft/201m ⚠ **Difficulty** 2
Paths Woodland paths (sometimes muddy), tracks, 5 stiles
Map OS Explorer 219 Wolverhampton & Dudley **Grid ref** SO 938807
Parking National Trust pay-and-display car park, Nimmings Wood

❶ Walk to car park entrance, turn **R** and continue for few paces. Cross road to stile and take **L-H** option. Immediately you'll see striking urban panorama. Descend steadily but, at cylindrical wooden post in 2nd field, turn **R** (with waymarker). Continue across fields, probably populated with horses, to kissing gate. Here take forward option (not **R** fork), to reach churchyard of St Kenelm's in Romsley parish.
❷ Leave by lychgate. Turn **L** along road for short distance, then **R** at T-junction. In about 125yds (114m), take waymarked path at driveway to The Wesleys to ascend gently. Move **L** to find gate on to tarmac road. Turn **L**. Ignore **L** turn but, just 30yds (27m) beyond it, take muddy, gated narrow path into woodland up on **R**, angled away from road and not signposted. Emerge from trees to trig point on Walton Hill. Turn **L**, taking **R-H** of 2 options. Follow this for 0.75 mile (1.2km) until **R-H** fork leads to seen stile out of trees. Go

steeply down 2 meadows to road beside Church of St Leonard's in Clent.
❸ Turn **R** then **R** again, along Vine Lane. At Church View Cottage, opposite church's driveway, turn **L**. (Please follow these woodland directions especially carefully!) In 180yds (165m), take upper, **L** fork. In 80yds (73m), at crossing, go **L**. After further 100yds (91m) ignore options to turn **R** or half **R**. Proceed for 160yds (146m). Ignore gate and stile on **L** to go straight on, ascending steeply up wooden steps. Soon emerge from trees. Now cross track then turn **R**.
❹ Keep on this broad, open path, ignoring **R** fork, to reach semi-circular, 5-panel toposcope. From this take initially level path ahead, directly back to car park.

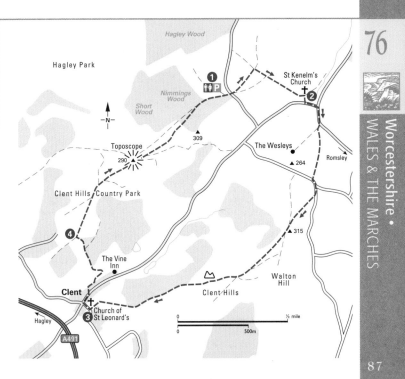

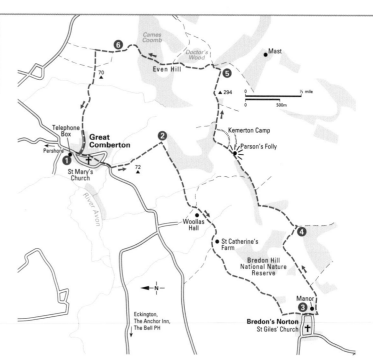

BREDON HILL Perry Country
A walk through perry country.

7.5 miles/12.1km 3hrs 45min **Ascent** 1,115ft/340m **Difficulty** 2
Paths Tracks, woodland paths, bridleways, minor lanes, 9 stiles **Map** OS Explorer 190 Malvern Hills & Bredon Hill **Grid ref** SO 953423 **Parking** Roadside parking, Great Comberton village

❶ Begin beside telephone box in Great Comberton. Follow Church Street. Cross churchyard; leave by old iron kissing gate. At road, go down '11%' gradient. In dip find stile. Ascend 2 fields, with stream on **L-H** side. In 3rd field, find (wobbly) signpost after 90yds (82m).
❷ Turn **R**, initially beside trees. Soon good farm track strikes across meadow. Follow waymarkers for 1.5 miles (2.4km), taking gravel driveway beside Woollas Hall and skirting St Catherine's Farm. Take hard track, later tarmac, down into Bredon's Norton. After first few houses, reach junction.
❸ Keep ahead for 100yds (91m) to junction. Turn **R** if visiting St Giles' Church; otherwise go ahead again, then round **L** bend. Go into field, to **R** of 2 buildings – there's waymarker on telegraph pole. Now follow excellent track steadily upwards, through gates, eventually swinging southeast, for at least 0.75 mile (1.2km). Less than 100yds (91m) beyond single marker post reach T-junction with 'no right of way' ahead.

❹ Turn **L**, shortly veering **R** along field edge. Ascend for 600yds (549m), then turn **R** to walk along wooded escarpment ridge, before open field leads to Parson's Folly on edge of Kemerton Camp. Follow escarpment eastwards, keeping wall on **L** to reach small conifer plantation. Just past this, ignore downward fork, instead following wire fence for over 0.25mile (400m), to wood.
❺ Turn **L**, beside wood. Within 150yds (137m), bend **R** to junction. Turn **L**, down green hollow. At Doctor's Wood veer **L** to cross level field, Even Hill. Find stile hidden in dip. Descend steeply through Cames Coomb, along wide, well-horsed path. Briefly follow level forestry road; leave trees, descending on track for 400yds (366m) to metal kissing gate on **R**.
❻ Walk 275yds (251m) on good track to find path on **L**, initially between 2 hedges. When it ends, go ahead. Keep this general line – later hard track – back into Great Comberton. Turn **R** to telephone box.

WORCESTER CITY Sights And Smells

A town walk in Worcester, known for Sir Edward Elgar, its porcelain, its racecourse and its sauce.

2.5 miles/4km 1hr 30min **Ascent** Negligible ⚠ **Difficulty** ☐1
Paths City streets and tarmac riverside path **Map** OS Explorer 204 Worcester & Droitwich Spa
Grid ref SO 846548 **Parking** Long-stay pay-and-display car parks at New Road, Tybridge Street and Croft Road (and elsewhere)

❶ Route begins at city side of road bridge, but you can pick it up anywhere – at The Commandery or the Guildhall, for example – depending on where you have parked. Turn **L**, passing The Old Rectifying House (wine bar). Turn **R** after Severn View Hotel, then **L**, in front of bus station, following road round to pass The Butts Dig (archaeological site). Turn **L** along Farrier Street, **R** into Castle Street, reaching northern extremity of route at its junction with Foregate Street.
❷ Go **R** along Foregate Street, passing Shire Hall and Worcester City Art Gallery & Museum. Continue along The Cross and into pedestrianised area called High Street. Turn **L** into Pump Street. (Elgar's statue stands close to his father's piano shop, at southern end of High Street.) Turn **L** again, into The Shambles. At junction turn **R** into Mealcheapen Street. Another **R** turn and you're in New Street (later becomes Friar Street).

❸ Head down this partial time warp as slowly as you can, admiring The Greyfriars (National Trust property) in particular, for dual carriageway awaits you at end. Turn **R**, then cross over carefully, to visit cathedral.
❹ Leave the cathedral along College Precincts to fortified gateway known as Edgar Tower. (It is named after the 10th-century King Edgar, but was actually built in the 14th century. Go through this gateway to see College Green.) Continue, along what is now Severn Street, which, unsurprisingly, leads to River Severn. Turn **R**, to complete your circuit, by following Kleve Walk, leafy waterside avenue; this section floods frequently, as does county cricket ground opposite at great cost to club's revenue.

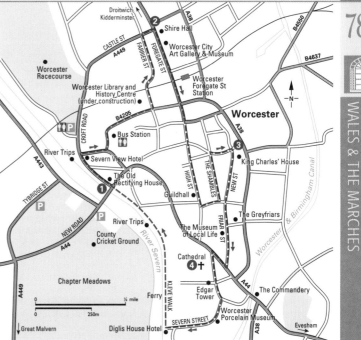

KINGSFORD Country Park And Villages

A backwater that once knew busier times.

5.5 miles/8.8km 2hrs 30min **Ascent** 410ft/125m ⚠ **Difficulty** 1

Paths Forest rides, meadows, minor roads, village streets, canal towpath, 9 stiles
Map OS Explorer 218 Wyre Forest & Kidderminster or 219 Wolverhampton & Dudley
Grid ref SO 835820 **Parking** Blakeshall Lane car park, Kingsford Forest Park

❶ Take track inside northern edge of forest park for 550yds (503m), to point about 80yds (73m) beyond end of Kinver Edge Farm's garden. To **L** is wide glade, falling gently; ahead rises woodland track.

❷ Turn **L**, down ride. In 275yds (251m), at 5-way junction, go ahead (not along slight **R** fork). Join farm track. At road turn **R**, through Blakeshall. After 300yds (274m), at **R-H** bend near power lines, take stile into field. Keep hedge on **R**, following yellow waymarkers into small valley. When about 300yds (274m) from Debdale Farm, move up to fence, following it to corner. Enter Gloucester Coppice at gate and stile. Follow this track, soon more defined, to southern end of Blakeshall Lane.

❸ Turn **L**, descending into Wolverley. See footbridge alongside The Queen's Head and The Old Village Store, but take other one. Reach Church of St John the Baptist by iron gates, zig-zagging up concreted footpath through deep cutting (if gates are locked use

road). Leave churchyard by modern steps. Go down meadow opposite (with fingerpost) to minor road.

❹ Turn **R**. At B4189, turn **L**. In front of The Lock public house turn **L**, along towpath. After about 1.25miles (2km) is Debdale Lock, partly hewn into rock. Some 220yds (201m) further, just before steel wheel factory, is stile.

❺ Turn **L** here along track. At T-junction after coniferous avenue, turn **R** on broad gravel track. After about 350yds (320m) turn **L** (waymarker), up wooden steps, into trees. Go up **L-H** edge of 1 field and centre of another to road. Turn **L** for just 15yds (14m), then **R**. Some 400yds (366m) along this hedged lane turn **R**, contrary to blue arrow pointing ahead. At next stile wiggle **L**, then **R**. Proceed ahead at junction to road. Turn **R**. In 150yds (137m), move **L** into trees to re-enter country park. 2 paths run parallel to road – both lead back to car park.

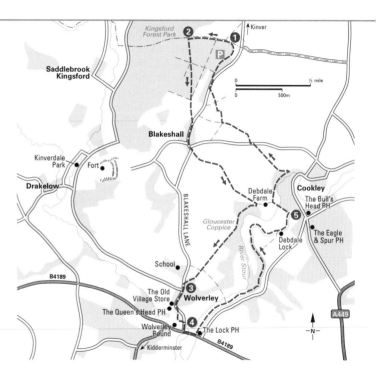

MARTLEY Through the Cider Orchards

A marvellous, airy stretch of countryside.

7 miles/11.3km 3hrs 15min **Ascent** 720ft/219m ⚠ **Difficulty** 2

Paths Field paths, lanes, orchard paths, tracks, river meadows, minor roads, 16 stiles
Map OS Explorer 204 Worcester & Droitwich Spa **Grid ref** SO 756597 **Parking** St Peter's Church, Martley

❶ Go through churchyard to B4204. Cross to track. In 100yds (91m) walk in trees, parallel to school. Turn **R** into field, then re-enter grounds. Briefly follow **L** edge of playing fields; gate gives on to field. At road, turn **L**. Turn **R**, signposted 'Highfields'. Beside Lingen Farm go down track. At bend take stile, straight across field. Cross stream, then ascend, taking **R-H** gates to minor road.
❷ Turn **L**. At Larkins go ahead, taking 2 stiles then field path, not inviting parallel gravel track. Go ahead for 2 fields; at red sign, don't move **R**, but forge on, squeezing past breeze block barn and driveway of white bungalow, to walk behind Ross Green's gardens. Cross fields to road. Go over to partially concealed stile, not diagonally to prominent fingerpost. Walk beside barn, then in next field skirt **L** to lane. Turn **R** for few paces to fingerpost pointing into apple orchard before Peartree Cottage.
❸ Follow waymarkers carefully through this vast orchard, descending gently. Emerge at bridge over ditch, beside apple-sorting equipment. Go 200yds (183m) up track, to gap in evergreens. Turn **L**, down orchard ride. At T-junction turn **R**, up to just before gate beside house.

Turn **L**, almost back on yourself. Go carefully through orchard, following faded yellow splodges about 1.5ft (45cm) up on tree trunks, but sometimes obscured by branches. Leave by footbridge, crossing fields to B4197.
❹ Turn **R** for 60yds (55m). Take excellent track (mostly tarmac) for 0.5 mile (800m) to Rodge Hill's top. Turn sharp **L**, 'Worcestershire Way'. Follow this for 1 mile (1.6km). Steps lead down to road's hairpin bend.
❺ Turn **R**. In 20yds (18m) turn **L**, but in only 15yds (14m) turn **R** again, into conifers. Emerge to drop steeply. At B4204 turn **R** for 30yds (27m). Use permissive path across 2 fields to River Teme. Follow this riverside walk, later in Kingswood Nature Reserve, for over 0.5 mile (800m). Leave river when wire fence requires it. Ascend path, later driveway, to tarmac road.
❻ Turn **R**, uphill; this soon bends **L**. Near brow move **R** (waymarker) just to walk in field, not on road. At tarmac junction turn **L** but, in 275yds (251m), walk beside a wire fence. Beside fields and allotments, emerge between Crown and garage. Pass telephone box into village, then turn **R** to the church at start.

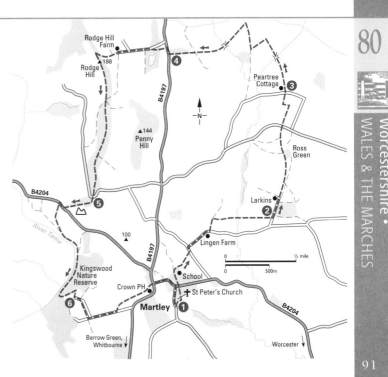

DROITWICH SPA Salt Into Silver *An historic salt-making town.*

5.75miles/9.2km 2hrs 30min **Ascent** 230ft/70m ⚠ **Difficulty** 1

Paths Pavements, field paths, stony tracks, 5 stiles

Map OS Explorer 204 Worcester & Droitwich Spa **Grid ref** SO 898631 **Parking** Long-stay pay-and-display between Heritage Way and Saltway (follow brown signs for Brine Baths)

1 Begin outside library with your back to Raven Hotel. Go west, along Victoria Square. Cross Heritage Way into Ombersley Street East. At bend go straight on, past medical centre. After underpass proceed to church. Go beyond churchyard then **R**; take underpass. Turn **L**. Take road over railway to mini-roundabout, filter **R**, go through 3rd underpass. Walk to fence corner, near lamppost. Turn **L**. In 30yds (27m) turn **R**. At bottom of this cul-de-sac, Westmead Close, turn **L**. Soon take Ledwych Close, on R. Reach canal.

2 Turn **L**. At bridge turn **R**, passing sports facilities and schools. Turn **L** just beyond A38 bridge, into Westwood Way. Reach Westwood House slip road. Facing allotments, take gate to **L**. Beyond woodland reach driveway. Cross arable field. Over track and driveway, reach corner of Nunnery Wood.

3 Turn sharp **R**. Electric fencing guides you between paddocks; veer **L** to walk briefly through Nunnery Wood. (Ignore tracks **L**.) Aim for 2 gates beside trees on skyline. Keep straight on for 0.5 mile (800m), near

Robert Wiseman Dairies on **L**, then curving **L** past industrial estate to Doverdale Lane.

4 Turn **R**. Just before '30' speed-limit sign, fork **L**. Cross A442. Walk through Hampton Lovett to St Mary's Church. Take meadow path under railway. In 140yds (128m), at footbridge, bear **R**, along field edge. Follow this waymarked line for 0.5 mile (800m), walking outside **R** edge of trees beside Highstank Pool. Go forward with hedgerow **L**; when it stops abruptly aim across field to clip to corner greenery.

5 Cross vast field to metal gate. Aim slightly **L** to another metal gate. Follow road under A38 into housing estate. Go forward, then down for 150yds (137m), to find tarmac path between Nos 49 and 53 (51 is hidden). Enter 2 kissing gates flanking level crossing. Turn **L** to The Gardeners Arms. Here turn **R** over river, into Vines Park. Veer **L** to cross Droitwich Canal. Cross busy road and walk down **R** side of supermarket to High Street. Ahead is Spats Coffee House. Turn **R**, passing Tower Hill, then **L** into St Andrew's Street and then back to start.

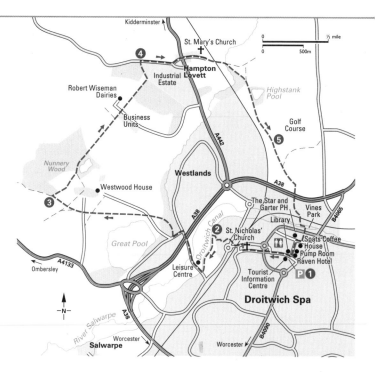

OMBERSLEY Along The River Severn

Explore an estate park.

5.75miles/9.2km 2hrs 30min **Ascent** 200ft/61m ⚠ **Difficulty** ☐1

Paths Riverside paths, field paths and tracks, village street, 6 stiles

Map OS Explorer 204 Worcester & Droitwich Spa **Grid ref** SO 845630 **Parking** Towards southern end of road through Ombersley on eastern side (no southbound exit from village)

❶ To south of village, beyond cricket ground, take path on **R**, signposted 'Turn Mill'. This is Wychavon Way. Briefly in trees, walk across meadow to stile beside willow. Go along **L-H** field edges, and briefly by water's edge. At corner of fish pond go few paces beyond waymarker to track. Turn **L**, following this track **R** in 80yds (73m). It becomes sunken path through delicious woodland. Cross a meadow to river.

❷ Turn right. In 0.75 mile (1.2km) you'll pass 2 fishing pools to reach Holt Fleet Bridge. Go under this, continuing for 1 mile (1.6km), passing staffed Holt Lock. Opposite The Lenchford Inn reach riverside stile.

❸ Don't cross stile; instead, turn **R**. In field corner join access road. At junction go ahead on public road. In 650yds (594m), at **R-H** bend, keep this line by moving **L**, on to farm track. It's over 0.25 mile (400m) to top of field. Keep on track seeing rusty shed ahead. 30yds (27m) before it, turn **R**. Now, in 90yds (82m) go **L**, through gate.

❹ What could be golf course fairway turns out to be enormous garden. Aim to pass **R** of house (Greenfields), and children's wooden watchtower, walking beside walled vegetable garden. Keep ahead down its private, brick-paved driveway. Turn **R**, passing black-and-white houses, to T-junction – Uphampton House is ahead.

❺ Turn **L** for 110yds (100m), then turn **R**, uphill. In 150yds (137m), at The Hollies, don't bend **R** but go ahead, on shingly track. About 220yds (201m) further, main track bends **R**, rough track goes ahead and public footpath goes half **L**.

❻ Take public footpath option, along field edge. Continue through small area of market garden, reaching cul-de-sac. Shortly turn **R**, along village street. Return to your car.

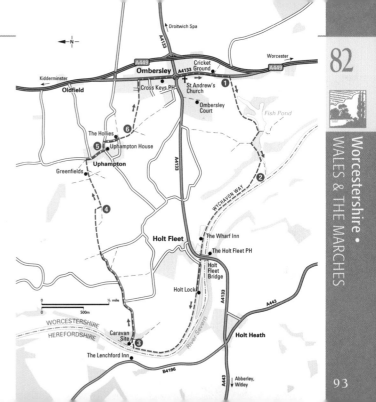

STOURPORT-ON-SEVERN Hartlebury Common

A Georgian 'new town' and a common.

3.25 miles/5.3km 1hr 30min **Ascent** 328ft/100m ⚠ **Difficulty** 1

Paths Towpath, tracks, good paths, some streets **Map** OS Explorer 218 Wyre Forest & Kidderminster or 219 Wolverhampton & Dudley **Grid ref** SO 820704 **Parking** Hartlebury Common South Car Park on A4025 (poorly signed; a white height restriction bar spans narrow entrance)

❶ Cross A4025. Turn **L** for just 25yds (23m) to take footpath. Strike across this bottom part of Hartlebury Common: you'll see buildings in far distance. Veer **R**, roughly following power lines, through silver birches, to find sandy track at back of houses. At modern housing estate join tarmac briefly, aiming for dirt track beyond 'Britannia Gardens' sign and after Globe House. Turn **L** down tarmac footpath, with wooden paling **L**, to river. ❷ Turn **R**. In 650yds (594m) reach lock and Stourport's canal basins. Route is neither across 2-plank walkway at upper lock gate, nor upper brick bridge; instead take neat brick-paved path to circumnavigate The Tontine. Now skirt Upper Basin, passing Limekiln Chandlers. Across York Street join towpath. Follow this for little under 0.75 mile (1.2km), leaving it at Bird in Hand, before defunct railway bridge. ❸ Go down Holly Road, then half **L** into Mill Road, following it for 0.25 mile (400m), over mini-roundabout and across River Stour to B4193. Cross and go to **L** of De

Rosa Glass to take narrow, sandy, uphill path back on to common. Soon, at fork, go **L**, keeping in this direction as ground levels and parking area lies **L**. Go ahead to find, adjacent to wire fence, unpainted trig point. ❹ Now retrace your steps for 90yds (82m), passing wooden waymarker, to junction. Here turn **L**, away from car park. Again in about 90yds (82m), at T-junction with marker post, turn **L** (signposted 'Heather Trail'). At corner of conifer plantation, 275yds (251m) further, turn **R**. After 100yds (91m) turn **L**, then in 220yds (201m), just after far end of plantation, enjoy views west. 65yds (60m) beyond viewpoint, take **R** option at subtle fork. Go forward on this for another 250yds (229m), to opening. Here step carefully over 2 exposed and disused (but not actually hazardous) pipes. Follow sandy track slanting downhill for 110yds (100m), then swing **R**, now making beeline for car park.

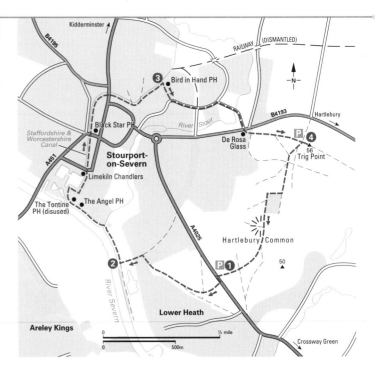

GREAT WITLEY Among The Trees

A woodland walk up and down some hills.

4.75 miles/7.7km 2hrs 30min **Ascent** 1,150ft/350m ⚠ **Difficulty** ②
Paths Woodland paths, field paths, tracks, 12 stiles
Map OS Explorer 204 Worcester & Droitwich Spa **Grid ref** SO 752662
Parking Large car park of The Hundred House Hotel
(as a courtesy please phone beforehand, tel 01299 896888)

❶ Cross A451 with great care. Through opening, strike sharp **R**, aiming for hedge end beside last house. Turn **L** on this lane. Walk for 0.5 mile (800m) along here, soon passing Walsgrove Farm and then (most of year) thousands of strutting, wailing geese. Do not turn **R** up lane but go half **R**, taking path that becomes beautiful wooded avenue, to top of Woodbury Hill. Reach 2nd information board.

❷ Go forward few paces to turn **R** at marker post. In 50yds (46m), turn **R**. Continue forward along inside edge of wood. Skirt to **L** of buildings at Birch Berrow, resuming on gravel, fenced-in path. Take 2 stiles. Go steeply down, taking stile into thick pines. In pasture again, descend further, reaching The Woodlands' driveway and T-junction. Turn **R** along road for 75yds (69m) to marker post just past 1 Hillside Cottages.

❸ Turn **R** again, back uphill. Continue north for nearly 1 mile (1.6km), with stiles and gates, walking

mostly in trees but later enjoying fine views west. Then, on top of Walsgrove Hill, you'll see magnificent clock tower (1883) of Abberley Hall. Now go steeply down this meadow, to take stile into lane. Turn **R** to B4203.

❹ Cross carefully. Turn **L**, along verge. Take driveway to Abberley Hall School. Leave driveway as it swings **R**, keeping this direction close to clock tower on track to A443. Take road opposite, 'Wynniattes Way', up to brow of hill.

❺ Turn **R**. In about 400yds (366m), reach trig point. Walk along ridge path further 650yds (594m) to Worcestershire Way sign at path junction, just beyond which are 4 trees growing in line across path.

❻ Take path down to **R**, initially quite steeply then contouring as it veers **R**, later descending again. Emerge from woods over stile to walk down 2 large fields meeting road beside The Hundred House Hotel.

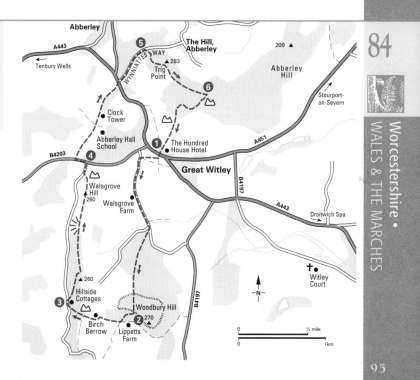

MAMBLE A Long Amble

Beside the Leominster Canal.

4.25 miles/6.8km 2hrs 15min **Ascent** 625ft/190m ⚠ **Difficulty** 1

Paths Minor roads, field and woodland paths, 11 stiles **Map** OS Explorer 203 Ludlow

Grid ref SO 685712 **Parking** Lay-by (bend in old road) west of Mamble on A456

❶ Go to Tenbury Wells end of lay-by. Take gate nearest road; go down **L-H** field edge. At woodland turn **R**, soon entering it by stile. Go forward at 2-plank bridge. In 200yds (183m) cross pastures to track by white house. ❷ Turn **L** for 75yds (69m). At gate move **R** on rising woodland track. At corner stay in trees, along path. Fork **R** shortly before fence. At this, ascend gently on **R** fork (waymarker), aiming 50yds (46m) **L** of skyline oak. At top turn **R**, following field edge to gate beside pond. ❸ Keep this line for 250yds (229m) to stile on **L**, shortly before corner. Climb this but don't follow waymarker forward and down; instead go through gate to **R**, and continue with this field edge on **R**. In next one go directly under large pylon to another stile. Walk initially with wire fence on **L**, but, within 30yds (27m) of hedgerow beginning, go through stile, putting this hedgerow on **R**. Reach 7-bar metal gate, one short field before cherry orchard. ❹ Do not go through; instead turn three-quarters around, to go diagonally down field, in search of stile

(perhaps concealed by bracken edge) nearly 100yds (91m) **L** of old metal gate. Enter orchard, skirting **R-H** perimeter. Just few paces around orchard's bottom corner leave by stile. Move **R** few paces to wooden post; here fork **L** (not uphill). In 50yds (46m) go through metal gate and see footbridge down **L**. Across this turn **L** (waymarker), along little-used path, to minor road. ❺ Turn **L**. Keep ahead at junction, then ascend sharply, and drop down past 'Frith Common' sign. Keep ahead at next crossroads too. Now you have another pull up, but, before red telephone box, beside entrance to Rose Cottage and The Observatory, take narrow path. Soon in field, follow **L-H** edge to stile. Strike half **R** (waymarked), descending 2 pastures easily to walk beside woodland on **L**. Gate leads you down to Stocking Pool. ❻ Cross dam to gate. Turn **L** for 350yds (320m), until woodland is ahead. Move **R** perhaps 40yds (37m) to stile (not 2nd further **R**). Over this turn **L**. In 70yds (64m), cross avenue diagonally. A waymarker leads you across fields to gate. Through this return to car park.

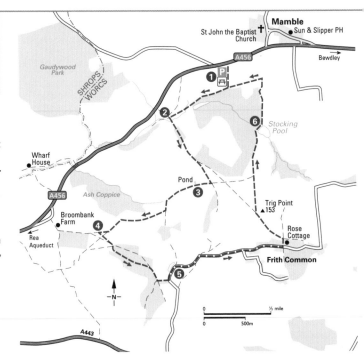

PREES Branching Out from Prees

An exploration of Whixall Moss, together with two branches of the Shroppies.

10 miles/16.1km 3hrs 30min **Ascent** 98ft/30m ⚠ **Difficulty** ③

Paths Some road walking (take care on blind bends on Post Office Lane), about 20 stiles (some in disrepair) **Map** OS Explorer 241 Shrewsbury **Grid ref** SJ 537337

Parking Where bridleway meets lane by Prees Station, take care not to block access

❶ Join bridleway by signal box. Soon ignore blocked stile, use gate near by. Enter field and follow **R-H** edge to stile. Cross to other side of hedge, but continue in same direction. Keep on across 4 fields to B5476.

❷ Walk along road opposite (signed 'Whixall') and straight on at 2 junctions. Take care here. Turn **R** by Whixall Social Centre, then **L** on to driveway before Church Farm.

❸ At Farthing Cottage, turn **R**. Cross field, passing pond, then continue across next field. Go slightly **L** across 3rd field to 2 stiles and footbridge. Don't cross, but go through gate, **L**, opening into large field. Turn **L**, keeping about 100yds (91m) from its **L-H** edge. At 3 large oaks, go diagonally **R** to gate and then cross another field to lane.

❹ Turn **R**, then **L** at junction and straight on at next. Join 1st path on **R** after Whixall School. Cross 3 fields to Llangollen Canal and cross Roundthorn Bridge, then turn **R** to information board telling you about NNR. Take

leaflet from box (acts as permit to enter reserve). In few paces turn **L**, following orange-coded Mosses Trail.

❺ At Point ⑧ on trail, turn **L** to meet canal at Morris' Bridge. Turn **R** on towpath to canal junction, then cross Roving Bridge to join Prees Branch. Towpath changes sides at Dobson's Bridge. Beyond Whixall Marina canal is disused and has become Shropshire Wildlife Trust nature reserve.

❻ Meet lane at Waterloo Bridge. Turn **L**, then immediately **R**, signposted 'Edstaston'. Keep straight on past Abbeygreen turning, but turn **L** at T-junction and follow lane into Edstaston.

❼ Just before church go through gate on **L**; 2nd gate and then stile into field. Go across this to B5476. Turn **L**, then cross to lane. Follow it past Edstaston Hall and couple of farms. Turn **L** on bridleway (sign overgrown). In 300m (274yds) bear **R** to gate and continue to railway. Follow it north, bearing slightly **L** to join clear track back to Prees Station.

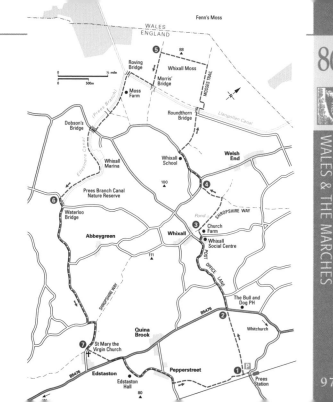

MARKET DRAYTON A Sweet-Toothed Town

Enjoy a veritable feast of gingerbread men and Cheshire cheese.

5.25 miles/8.4km 2hrs **Ascent** 165ft/50m ⚠ **Difficulty** 1

Paths Streets, towpath, sandy track and quiet lanes; field paths and 9 stiles

Map OS Explorer 243 Market Drayton **Grid ref** SJ 674344

Parking Car park on Towers Lawn, next to bus station

❶ Walk past bus station, cross at zebra crossing, then turn **L** down Queen Street to Buttercross and **L** on Stafford Street. Go straight on at 1st junction, **R** at next on to Great Hales Street and then **L** on Berrisford Road (use easily missed footway on L until forced to join road).

❷ You'll soon come to Berrisford Bridge, also known as 40 Steps Aqueduct, which carries Shropshire Union Canal over road. Go up steps and turn **R** on towpath. This part of Shroppie system was originally Birmingham and Liverpool Junction Canal, which went from Autherley to Nantwich. Thomas Telford was the engineer and the boldness of his design is apparent along this stretch, with its massive cuttings and embankments. The deep cutting on the approach to Tyrley Locks has its own microclimate, and positively drips with ferns, mosses and liverworts. The towpath marks the county boundary – this stretch of the canal is in Staffordshire.

❸ At bridge 60 by Tyrley Wharf go up to lane (Tyrley Road) and turn **R**. This leads to main road (A529) and pub called The Four Alls. Cross with care to Sandy Lane.

❹ Sandy Lane comes to T-junction with track. Turn **R** here; it's still Sandy Lane, but this part is private road and dogs must be kept on a lead. It heads north towards Drayton, overlooked by Salisbury Hill, where a Yorkist army under the Earl of Salisbury camped in 1459 before heavily defeating a Lancastrian force twice the size.

❺ When you meet road, turn **R** to cross River Tern at Walkmill Bridge (packhorse bridge). Cross wider road and go up Kilnbank Road opposite. Where it ends turn **R**. After passing Sandbrook Vaults, turn **L** past Buttercross to Cheshire Street, which leads back to Towers Lawn.

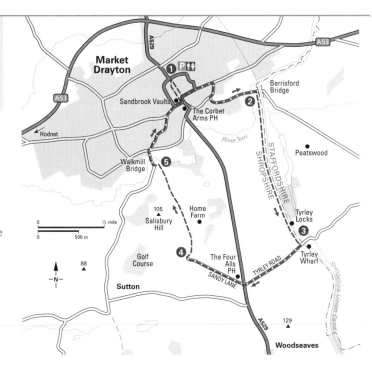

BRIDGNORTH Up Jacob's Ladder

Sheer cliffs and secluded valleys.

6.5 miles/10.4km 2hrs 30min **Ascent** 540ft/165m ⚠ **Difficulty** ②

Paths Steep and eroded in parts (beware landslips), 1 stile
Map OS Explorer 218 Wyre Forest & Kidderminster **Grid ref** SO 720934
Parking Severn Park, off A442 on east bank of Severn at Bridgnorth

❶ Cross A442, turn **L**, then **R**, signed 'cemetery'. At cemetery take footpath, **L**, climbing steeply. The gradient eases: turn **R** on fenced path, then climb again through woods. At top keep **L** to waymarked junction.

❷ Fork **L**, descending before path (Jacob's Ladder) levels to contour in undulating fashion round High Rock and Pendlestone Rock. At junction, keep to higher path, which soon swings **R**. Leaving trees, it passes Woodside Farm, then merges with farm access track.

❸ Meeting lane, turn **R** for few paces, then **L** at footpath sign. Pass house and go through gate into field. Proceed along edge almost to end, then turn **R** to a gate opposite. Turn **L** into narrow field and descend in bottom of valley.

❹ Meet track by sandstone building and turn **R** along steep-sided valley. Where main track bends **R**, keep on along grassy path through bracken. Eventually reach junction with sandy track beside River Worfe.

❺ Onward route is to **R**, but first it's worth short detour **L** to explore lovely hamlet of Rindleford. Resuming walk, return to junction and follow sandy track, first by river then swinging **R** to climb gently out of valley.

❻ Turn **R** at lane. After 600yds (549m) turn **L** at waymarked gate and follow footpath along field edge. This leads to A454 and continues on other side, past housing estate (The Hobbins).

❼ Turn **R** on another road, which runs past Stanmore Country Park, to A454. Cross to track opposite, by Hermitage Farm. Follow track round **R** at top. As you approach metal gates, go through hedge gap and continue along narrow path, always close to edge of wood. Audibly nearing B4363, look for parallel path on **L**, which descends past The Hermitage. Cross road to footpath opposite and follow this, with steep slopes on **L**, until sharp **L** turn takes you back down past cemetery to A442 and Severn Park.

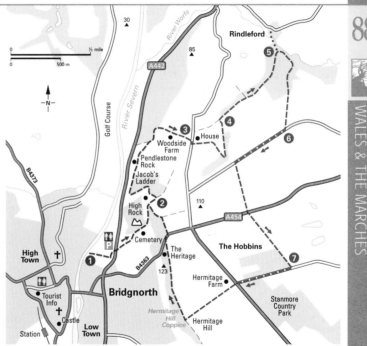

WYRE FOREST The King's Wood
A leafy walk in Wyre Forest.

5 miles/8km 2hrs 30min **Ascent** 575ft/175m ⚠ **Difficulty** 2
Paths Woodland and field paths, 4 stiles
Map Explorer 218 Wyre Forest & Kidderminster **Grid ref** SO 743784
Parking Forestry Commission car park at Earnwood Copse, on south side of B4194, west of Buttonoak

① Go through gate on forest road and immediately turn **R** on footpath into Earnwood Copse. Keep straight on at all junctions, eventually joining sunken path not far from edge of forest. Fork **L** to pass under overhanging yew tree and continue downhill.

② Path meets route of Elan Valley pipeline, bringing Welsh water to Birmingham. Turn **R** and cross footbridge on edge of forest, to **R** of pipeline. Walk up bank into arable fields and then uphill, keeping **L** of hedge. At top, go through hedge gap; turn **L**, soon recrossing hedge at waymarked gate. Stile in field corner leads to dark leafy tunnel, then clear track, which passes restored and extended cottage.

③ Soon reach T-junction at forest edge. Go few paces **L** towards Kingswood Farm then swing **R** on track into forest. Keep straight on at all junctions, descending steadily through Brand Wood.

④ Approaching Dowles Brook, don't cross; swing **L** on main track, just above it. Follow this for 1.25 miles

(2km), with Wimperhill Wood on **L**.

⑤ Turn **L** on bridleway, which crosses marshy area, then climbs through scrub and young woodland. It's waymarked and easily followed. Cross forest road, keep straight on, then turn **R** at next waymarked junction (post inconspicuous on **L**) before swinging **L** and down to bridge. Bridleway now climbs along rim of valley.

⑥ Reaching more open area, turn sharp **L** (still on bridleway). You're approaching Longdon Orchard now (conservation area; dog must be under control). At T-junction go **L**, into conifers; track immediately swings **R**. Follow it to waymarked junction; bridleway goes **R**.

⑦ Turn **R** when you meet Elan Valley pipeline again, then soon **L**, still on bridleway. Quickly fork **R**, on National Cycle Network Route 45. Follow it to edge of forest near Buttonoak, then turn **L** just before road to return to Earnwood Copse.

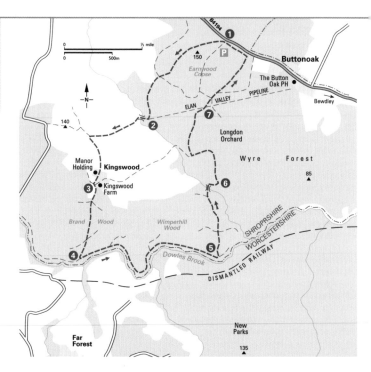

ELLESMERE Mosses And Moraines

A wonderful watery walk.

7.25 mile/11.7km 3hrs **Ascent** 180ft/55m ⚠ **Difficulty** ☐1
Paths Field paths and canal towpath, 8 stiles
Map OS Explorer 241 Shrewsbury **Grid ref** SJ 407344
Parking Castlefields car park opposite The Mere

❶ Cross to The Mere and turn **L**. Pass The Boathouse and Meres Visitor Centre and walk towards town, until you come to Cremorne Gardens. Join path that runs through trees close by water's edge for about 0.75 mile (1.2km).

❷ Ignore paths going **L** until you meet path signposted 'Welshampton'. Path soon joins track. Ignore **R** turn 'Private Road'. Just before Crimps Farm turn **R** on another track.

❸ Track leads into sheep pasture where you go straight on, guided by waymarkers and stiles. Go through field with pool in it and then aim for 3 prominent trees close together at far side. As you approach them, bear **L** into field corner.

❹ Go through gate and descend by **R-H** hedge. When it turns corner, go with it, to **R**. Skirt pool and keep going in same direction on grassy track, passing another pool. Track soon becomes much better defined and leads to farm where you join road.

❺ Turn **L** into Welshampton. Go past church and turn immediately **R** on Lyneal Lane. Follow it to bridge over Llangollen Canal. Descend steps to towpath and turn **R**, passing under bridge. Pass Lyneal Wharf, Cole Mere, Yell Wood and Blake Mere, then go through Ellesmere Tunnel. Beyond this are 3 footpaths signposted to The Mere. Take any of these short cuts, but to see more of canal, including the visitor moorings and marina, stay on towpath.

❻ Arriving at bridge 58, further choices present themselves. You could extend this walk to include signposted Wharf Circular Walk or to explore the town: just follow signs. To return directly to The Mere, however, go up to road and turn **R**.

❼ Fork **R** on road by lots of high walls. Turn **R** at top, then soon **L** at Rose Bank, up steps. Walk across earthworks of long-gone Ellesmere Castle and follow signs for The Mere or car park.

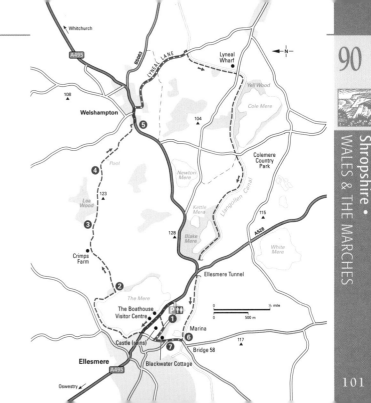

WHITTINGTON From Castle To Canal

Follow the Llangollen branch of the Shroppie through pastoral countryside.

6 miles/9.7km 2hrs 30min **Ascent** Negligible ⚠ **Difficulty** 2

Paths Towpath, lanes and field paths, some overgrown, 18 stiles

Map OS Explorer 240 Oswestry **Grid ref** SJ 325312

Parking Car park next to Whittington Castle – honesty box

❶ Cross pedestrian crossing in front of castle and follow Shrewsbury road (B5009), using footway on **L**. After 0.5 mile (800m), cross stile on **L** and follow waymarked path across 3 fields to corner by copse.

❷ Walk along field edge, with copse on **L**. Cross gap in corner, then go obliquely across another field following waymarker. Prominent oak tree is useful guide. There is gap near tree, but you may have cross nettles to get to it. In same direction cross next field to lane and turn **L**.

❸ Keep **L** at forks and continue to A495. Turn **R** for few paces, then cross to other side. Join footpath that runs along **L-H** field edge to stile and footbridge. Beyond these, keep going along field edge until hedge gap. Go through, then continue in same direction as before, soon going up bank.

❹ Meet canal at Pollett's Bridge (No 6). Join towpath and go under bridge. Follow towpath to Hindford Bridge (No 11), then go up to lane.

❺ Turn **R** past Jack Mytton Inn, then **R** again, signposted 'Iron Mills and Gobowen'. After 0.5 mile (800m), opposite no-through road, go **L** over stile. Walk down paddock to far end, then cross stile on **R**. Follow fence to footbridge, continue to another footbridge and keep straight on across marshy ground to stile ahead. Cross next field, aiming just **L** of copse. Go through gate and then **L** by field edge.

❻ Join track that soon bends **R** beside dismantled railway. Look out for stile giving access to railway. Turn **R** on former trackbed for few paces, then up bank on **L** – watch out for remains of steps concealed in undergrowth here. Cross stile to field, turn **R** to far side and cross another stile. Bear **L** to large oak tree, then continue to lane. Follow it to Top Street and turn **R**, then **L** to Whittington Castle.

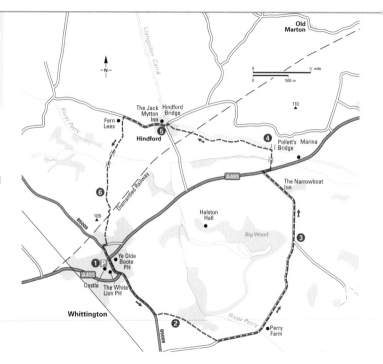

QUEEN'S HEAD The Full Monty At Queen's Head

A 19th-century canal village is one of the highlights along the restored Monty.

6.5 miles/10.4km 2hrs 30min **Ascent** 92ft/28m ⚠ **Difficulty** ☐1
Paths Towpath, quiet lanes and field paths, 10 stiles
Map OS Explorer 240 Oswestry **Grid ref** SJ 338268
Parking Car park at Queen's Head, between A5 and B5009

❶ Join towpath and head northeast, away from A5. Within few minutes you will approach Corbett's Bridge. About 50yds (46m) before it, look for stile hidden in hedge across road. Bear **R** across narrow damp meadow to another stile then continue on same heading over rise and down other side. Pass through gappy hawthorn hedge, then continue in same direction to far corner of field. Cross into another field, go forward few paces and turn **R** to road.

❷ Turn **L**, then **L** again, signposted 'Twyford'. Ignore Twyford turn little further on and instead continue to crossroads (Bishop's Corner). Turn **R** on School Road, then immediately **L** on grassy path (Hicksons Lane).

❸ Turn **L** on Old Holyhead Road, then 3rd **R** on Fox Lane, soon crossing A5 on footbridge. Go straight on through West Felton, then **L** on Woolston Road. OS map shows several footpaths, but many are obstructed so stick to road for nearly 1 mile (1.5km).

❹ After obvious double bend and just before cottage, cross stile on **R**. Follow line of garden hedge, straight across field to footbridge and 2 stiles. Cross boggy corner of next field and continue straight on to wobbly stile giving access to canal towpath. Turn **L**, soon passing under small bridge.

❺ Cross next bridge at Maesbury Marsh, and walk through village. Take 1st **R** turn, along Waen Lane – becomes public bridleway at cattle grid. Few paces further on, take footpath that leaves bridleway at gate on **R**. Head diagonally across large field to furthest corner, guided by waymarkers and vehicle track.

❻ Cross footbridge and continue over next field, then across stile to join bridleway. Keep straight on, passing **L** of house and along field edges until unsigned but trodden path goes **R**, to cross canal at small bridge you passed under at Point ❹. Descend steps on **R** and go under bridge to towpath. Follow it back to Queen's Head.

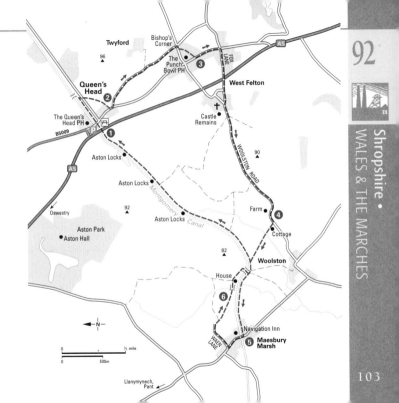

HOPE VALLEY
Hope For The Dormouses *Stunning countryside in the shadow of Stiperstones.*

9.5 miles/15.3km 3hrs 30min **Ascent** 1,279ft/390m ⚠ **Difficulty** 3

Paths Some boggy areas, streams to ford, route-finding skills required, 27 stiles

Map OS Explorer 216 Welshpool & Montgomery **Grid ref** SJ 350017

Parking Hope Valley Nature Reserve, signposted from A488

❶ Follow bridleway through reserve. Ignore branching paths; eventually meet lane. Turn **L**. Pass Stables Inn to 2 footpaths on **R**. Take **R-H** path, going forward to hedge corner; follow hedge to field corner.

❷ Follow next **L** field edge. Stiles lead to path down pasture. Cross brook by oak and follow track towards farm. Cross stile, turn **L;** follow waymarks to lane.

❸ Turn **L**, then 1st **R** on track to stile. Turn **R** along field edge, past cottage, until hedge turns corner. Cross field, climbing to stile/gate. Path continues across track and 2 more fields, then goes through copse to driveway. Turn **L** to lane, then **R**, keeping straight on along track.

❹ Cross lane and climb up Bromlow Callow. Enter fenced Scots pines on summit. Leaving trees, turn sharp **L** and descend, keeping **L** of thickest gorse, to marshy saddle. Below on **L** is stile. Descend **R**-wards to lane and cross to footpath. Follow along field edges and to lane.

❺ Descend through crossroads, towards Hopesgate. Turn 1st **R** on bridleway and follow it to T-junction, then go **L**. After The Brooklands it bears **L**, roughly following power lines, then becomes clearer track.

❻ At old quarry turn **L** down bank (uneven ground),

past fallen tree and across field. At far side muddy path drops **R** to brook. Turn **R** to see stile at other side; ford brook. Cross stile and turn **R** to footbridge across brook.

❼ Reach A488; cross to path opposite. Pass riding centre; follow fenced path past house to stile. Climb slope past 3 stiles. At crest, bear **L** and then descend confined path to Bank Farm.

❽ Cross lawn (waymarks); follow access track to lane. Turn **R**, then 1st **L** on bridleway. Bear slightly **R** across field to find metal gate; cross footbridge. Climb up to field. Bear **R**, woodland **L**, cross bridge, skirt Lower Santley farm; keep to field edge until way enters wood. Turn 2nd **R** on path, descending to Stiperstones.

❾ Turn **L**, past pub and shop, then **R** at Mytton Dingle. Enter gate, turn **L** into Stiperstones National Nature Reserve. Follow path round Oak Hill, then down to road. Cross to bridleway and turn **L**. Turn **R** at T-junction, through farmyard, then along track.

❿ At junction, turn **L** briefly, then **R** on footpath. Cross 4 fields; go **L** on track. Pass through gateway; turn **R**, following **R-H** hedge to gate. Turn **L** to A488 and cross to Hope Valley Nature Reserve.

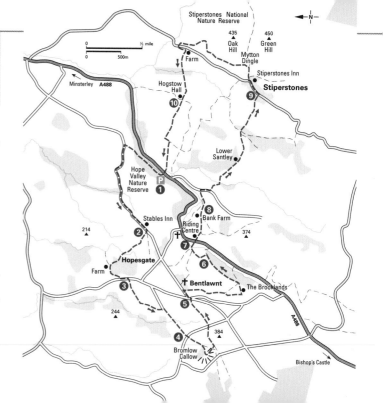

STIPERSTONES Back To Purple

From the mining village of Snailbeach to the dragon's crest of Stiperstones.

4.5 miles/7.2km 2hrs **Ascent** 951ft/290m ⚠ **Difficulty** 2
Paths Good paths across pasture, moorland and woodland
Map OS Explorer 216 Welshpool & Montgomery **Grid ref** SJ 374023
Parking Car park at Snailbeach

❶ Take Lordshill lane opposite car park, then join parallel footpath on **L**. Rejoining lane, cross to site of locomotive shed, then continue up lane, noticing green arrows directing you to main sites.

❷ Turn **R** on track between crusher house and compressor house. Few paces past compressor house, turn **L** up steps. At top, turn **R**, then soon **L** up more steps. Turn **L** to Cornish engine house, then **R** and continue through woodland. Detour leads to smelter chimney, or it's uphill all way.

❸ Sign indicates that you're entering Stiperstones National Nature Reserve (NNR). Woods give way to bracken, broom and bramble before gate leads to open hill. Path climbs slope ahead to stile/gate at top.

❹ 2 paths are waymarked. Take **L-H** one, which runs between fence and rim of spectacular dingle on **R**. Climbing away from dingle, bear **R** on grassy ramp before meeting rutted track. Turn **R**. As path climbs you can see rock tors on summit. Nearest, isolated from rest, is Shepherd's Rock.

❺ Just beyond Shepherd's Rock is junction marked by cairn. Turn **L** and after about 50yds (46m) fork **L** again. Descend to leave NNR at gate/stile. Path runs to **L**, shortly bordered by hawthorn hedge. This is old green lane, variously lined by trees or tumbledown stone wall. It runs through local nature reserve of Brook Vessons.

❻ Keep straight ahead at NNR sign. At next junction, fork **R** to leave NNR at gate by plantation. Go diagonally across field to track; turn **R**, going back across field, through plantation, then across pasture on bridleway.

❼ Fork **L** at bridleway junction and continue past Lordshill chapel to lane. Turn **R** and stay with it as it swings **L** to Snailbeach.

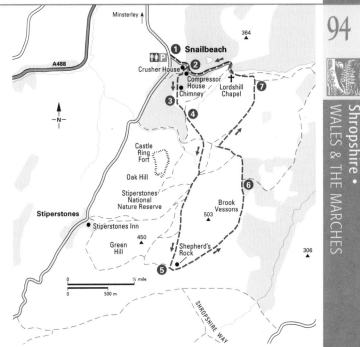

BISHOP'S CASTLE Life And Death

A colourful town.

7 miles/11.3km 2hrs 30min **Ascent** 738ft/225m ⚠ **Difficulty** 2
Paths Generally good, undefined across some fields, 13 stiles
Map OS Explorer 216 Welshpool & Montgomery **Grid ref** SO 324886
Parking Car park off Station Street

❶ Walk up Church Street, High Street and Bull Street, then go **L** along Bull Lane (B4385). At next junction bear **L** into new development of eco-homes, Wintles. Pass between 2 granite obelisks then go up steps on **R**, with wooden railings. Go **L** on green path, near road, then through hedge at footpath sign. Join green lane, and when it ends bear **L** to stile.

❷ Follow **R** edge of next field, cross stile at top and go slightly **L** to fence corner. Follow fence/hedge past pond to stile. Go slightly **L** across highest point of next field, then down to gate half-way along far hedge. Go diagonally **R** across another field to meet hedge and follow it along to track. Turn **L** to meet road.

❸ Turn **R**, **R** again and then **L** on to lane, which soon becomes track. It descends into woodland, crosses border into Wales and eventually meets lane.

❹ Turn **L** and walk up to meet road (Kerry Ridgeway) at Bishop's Moat, where you cross back into England. Turn **R**, then through 1st gate on **L**. Go diagonally **L** to

end of line of hawthorn trees, then continue in same direction over another field to meet far hedge where there's kink in it.

❺ Go diagonally across 3rd field to meet line of trees which leads to gate. Continue down next field to far corner, walking through scrap-metal.

❻ Meeting farm lane, turn **R** through farmyard at Upper Woodbatch and continue on down track to stile on **L**.

❼ Descend little further, now with hedge on **R**, then go **L** across field to gate at far side below steeper slope. Continue across 2 more fields to meet lane. Join Shropshire Way opposite, following it along bottom of several fields, quite close to brook.

❽ After passing abandoned quarry, turn **L** uphill opposite gate and track on **R**. Join track, then green path which leads to Field Lane. Follow this to Church Lane, which leads to Church Street and beginning of walk.

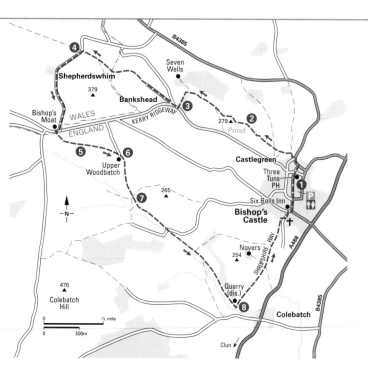

THE LONG MYND An Ancient Settlement

Prehistoric remains and magnificent views.

7.5 miles/12.1km 3hrs **Ascent** 1,545ft/471m ⚠ **Difficulty** ③

Paths Mostly moorland paths and tracks, 3 stiles
Map OS Explorer 217 The Long Mynd & Wenlock Edge **Grid ref** SO 453936
Parking Easthope Road car park, Church Stretton

❶ Walk up Lion Meadow to High Street and turn **R**. Turn **L** at The Square, go past church and straight on into Rectory Field. Walk to top **L** corner, then turn **R** along wall and go up into Old Rectory Wood. Path descends to junction, where you turn **R**, soon crossing Town Brook. Turn **L** and climb to gate on to Long Mynd.
❷ Go forward beside brook to meet iron railings, then continue in same direction with brook on **L**. After almost imperceptible height gain, path begins to climb more steeply and heads away from brook. Eventually path and brook meet up again near head of latter.
❸ Path crosses brook. Proceed 50yds (46m) to junction marked by 1st in succession of pink-banded posts. Just follow posts now, gaining height very gradually again. Ignore branching paths and, after ascending slight rise, you'll see summit ahead on **L**.
❹ Meet unfenced road about 100yds (91m) **L** of junction. Turn **L**, ignore paths to Townbrook and Little Stretton, and go straight on when road bends **L**, joining

bridleway. At next junction, turn **L** to summit, then keep straight on to Port Way. Turn **R** past site of Pole Cottage.
❺ Turn **L** on footpath, signposted to Little Stretton. It's wide rutted track; at fork go **L** – you can see path ahead, cutting green swath over shoulder of Round Hill. Go straight on at junction, then descend to Cross Dyke (Bronze Age earthwork). After dyke path ascends briefly, but soon levels out, then begins its descent, eventually following brook to Little Stretton.
❻ Cross at footbridge by ford and turn **R** on lane, but only for few paces. Look out for footpath on **L**. It climbs by field edge to top corner, then turns **L**, following top of steep slope to pasture. Follow **R-H** edge of this until path enters woodland. Descend to Ludlow Road.
❼ Immediately join bridleway next to footpath. It climbs into woodland. Emerge at far side to meet track, which soon becomes road. As it bends to **R** there's access **L** to Rectory Field. Descend to The Square, turn **R** on High Street and **L** on Lion Meadow to car park.

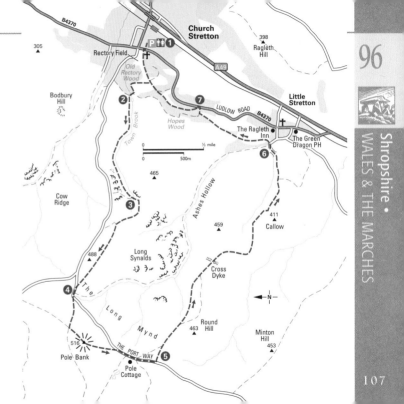

THE STRETTONS The Shapeliest Hills

If you like proper pointy hills, the exciting Strettons will make your day.

6 miles/9.7km 3hrs **Ascent** 1,060ft/323m **Difficulty** 2

Paths Good paths through pasture and woodland, 14 stiles

Map OS Explorer 217 The Long Mynd & Wenlock Edge **Grid ref** SO 453936

Parking Easthope Road car park, Church Stretton

1 Walk along road to Sandford Avenue and turn **R** past train station. Cross A49, proceed along Sandford Avenue, then turn **R** on Watling Street South. Turn **L** by postbox, fork **R** and shortly **L** on Ragleth Road.

2 Turn **R** into Woodland Trust reserve, Gough's Coppice. Keep **L** at fork, climbing by edge of wood, and **L** again at next junction. Leave wood at stile and turn **R** on footpath. After level section, path climbs steeply to stile. Turn **R** for few paces, then fork **L** to follow higher path, which goes by **L-H** fence through woodland.

3 When path emerges on to open hillside, keep straight on as far as stile, but don't cross it. Turn your back on it and follow trodden path up Ragleth Hill, then walk along spine of hill.

4 Pole marks southern summit. Descend steep well-worn path past rocks then follow fence down to stile. Drop **L** to another stile and climb to top **L** corner of next field. Go straight on to far **L** corner of another field and join lane.

5 Turn **L** and follow lane, with its wide flowery verge, for about 1 mile (1.6km), passing turn for Chelmick and Soudley.

6 Just past wooden house (Clemcroft) turn **L** on bridleway signed to Church Stretton. Follow this to gate and down through woodland.

7 Before 2nd gate turn **R** to contour round Hazler Hill. Turn **R** at lane, walk to junction and cross to bridleway opposite, which passes Gaerstones Farm. After Caer Caradoc comes into view, look for bridleway branching **L** to gate/stile about 40yds (37m) away. Bridleway descends past Helmeth Hill to meet another bridleway at point where this is crossed by brook.

8 Turn **L**, soon emerging from woodland into pasture. Keep on in much same direction, fence on **L**. Path becomes sunken track, which can be very muddy. Reaching lane, turn **L**. Turn **R** on Helmeth Road, **R** again at Sandford Avenue, and retrace outward route back to car park.

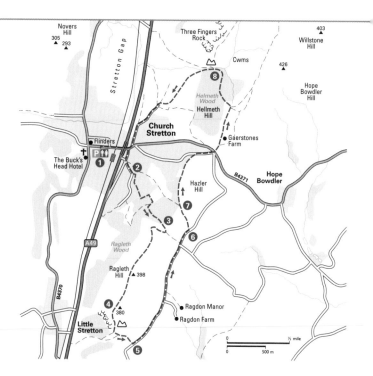

STOKESAY Over The Edge

A 13th-century house set in gorgeous hills.

6.25 miles/10.1km 2hrs 30min **Ascent** 909ft/277m △ **Difficulty** ②

Paths Mostly excellent, short stretch eroded and uneven, byway from Aldon to Stoke Wood occasionally floods, 13 stiles

Map OS Explorers 203 Ludlow; 217 The Long Mynd & Wenlock Edge

Grid ref SO 437819 (on Explorer 217) **Parking** Lay-by on A49 immediately north of Stokesay turn

❶ Take footway from lay-by to lane that leads to Stokesay Castle. Walk past castle and take 2nd footpath on **R**, at far side of pool. It skirts farm, then crosses railway. Keep straight on through 3 meadows on worn path, with stiles providing further guidance.

❷ Enter Stoke Wood, proceed to track and turn **R**. Leave wood at stile at far end and walk past house (Clapping Wicket) before turning sharp **L** up field in front of house. Turn **R** at top, walking by edge of View Wood.

❸ Join track that leads into wood, then emerges from it to run alongside edge. Where it seems vague, locate sunken track just inside wood, which climbs to stile, then meets lane by Viewedge Farm.

❹ Turn **L** for few paces, then join footpath on **R**. Turn **R** by field edge and walk to top of rise, continuing in same direction across fields until you come to waymarker that sends you sharp **L** across adjacent field. Join track at far side and continue past Gorst Barn to lane. Turn **R**.

❺ Turn **L** on footpath, crossing 3 pastures to concealed stile, which gives on to bridleway. Turn **L** down Brandhill Gutter. Opposite Brandy Bottom Cottage, go through gate on **R**, then immediately turn **L** to continue in same direction. Keep close to stream (often dry).

❻ After passing through gate, bridleway becomes narrow, uneven and eroded but soon improves. It eventually crosses stream (next to stile) and starts to swing northwards, into Aldon Gutter. Beyond abandoned cottage, keep **R** of pheasant pens to gate. Don't go through but follow hedge to **R**.

❼ Path becomes clear again, climbing steep valley side to meet lane at top. Turn **R** to pass through hamlet of Aldon, then **L** at T-junction.

❽ Join byway on **R** at slight bend in lane (no sign or waymarker). This lovely hedged track leads between fields, then descends through Stoke Wood, back to railway and lane past Stokesay Castle.

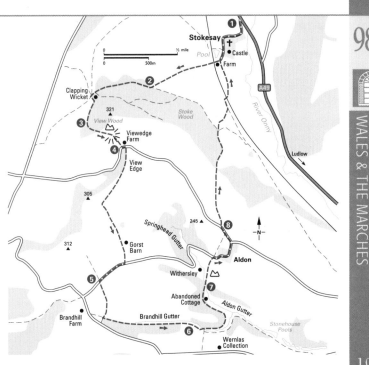

WART HILL Steaming Up Wart Hill

Great views from the hills, remembering the age of steam.

6 miles/9.7km 3hrs **Ascent** 918ft/280m **⚠ Difficulty** [2]

Paths Generally good, some muddy patches, steep, sometimes slippery descent from Wart Hill, about 20 stiles **Map** OS Explorer 217 The Long Mynd & Wenlock Edge **Grid ref** SO 430843

Parking Car park for Onny Trail, next to railway bridge on unclassified road from A49 to Cheney Longville

❶ Walk to lane and turn **R**. Keep ahead at junction and pass through Cheney Longville. At far side of village, fork **L** at sign for Castle Farm. Stony track passes farm and enters pasture.

❷ Walk along **R-H** field edge. In next field, go straight up slope. Path soon levels out and, little further on, waymarker sends you diagonally to bottom **R** field corner.

❸ Climb stile into woodland, walk to T-junction and turn **L**. Look for wobbly stile on **L**, or use nearby gate, and join track which runs past pool, then continues through plantation, soon swinging **L** and climbing. Go straight on at junction where permissive path goes **R**, and climb steeply to lane.

❹ Turn **R**, then **R** again after 500yds (457m) at sign (Wart Hill Wander). Few paces further on, turn **L** at signpost. Climb steeply through woodland to top of Wart Hill, covered in bracken, gorse and pines.

❺ Continue in same direction, past trig point, then follow waymarkers on steep descent, through conifers and then birch woods. Path rises and falls, twists and turns before turning **L** on stony track. At next track junction go **L**, then keep following waymarks.

❻ Meet lane, turn **L**, then immediately **R** on track into Heath Wood. At far side of wood, cross stile at junction and turn **R**. Track passes house (Middle Carwood), becoming vague as it climbs field then clear again at top **L** corner. It swings **R** and then **L** into woodland. Turn sharp **R** at T-junction near house.

❼ Brief climb through woods leads to junction. Turn **L**, descending steeply. Leaving trees, take narrow path through bracken to pass **L** of house, then keep going down, turning **R** where indicated. Path then hairpins down through hazel coppice to meet Onny Trail.

❽ Turn **R**, following waymarked trail. Pass 3 bridges spanning Onny. Continue to car park.

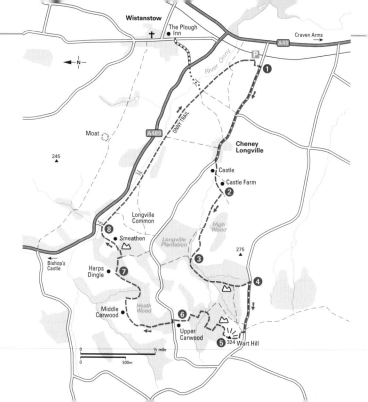

SUNNYHILL To Bury Ditches

Magnificent views from a dramatic hill fort.

5.5 miles/8.8km 2hrs **Ascent** 804ft/245m ▲ **Difficulty** ②

Paths Field and woodland paths, one boggy and overgrown, fence and gates to climb at Acton Bank,
8 stiles **Map** OS Explorer 216 Welshpool & Montgomery **Grid ref** SO 334839
Parking Forestry Commission car park at Sunnyhill off minor road north from Clunton

❶ From car park at Sunnyhill, walk back to lane and turn **L**. Descend through Lower Down and continue to Brockton. (If friendly lurcher adopts you here, be warned it is likely to follow you all the way round.) Turn **L** on track shortly before you come to ford. Pass buses in yard, then go through gate on **L** and walk along R-H edges of 3 fields, parallel with track.
❷ Climb over fence into wood then join track just below, contouring round base of Acton Bank. After leaving wood path continues through scrub, then through pasture below old quarries, before it meets lane in Acton.
❸ Turn **L**, pass to **R** of triangular green and join path running past White House Farm. Frequent waymarkers guide you past house, across field, then **L** over stile and along R-H edge of another field.
❹ Cross footbridge and continue straight across ensuing field towards building at far side. Cross stile

in hedge, turn **L** for few paces and then **R** on track, which passes by house (Brookbatch) and rises into woodland. When track eventually bends to **L**, go forward over stile instead and continue climbing.
❺ Emerging on to track, turn **L** past pond. Cross defunct cattle grid into Forestry Commission property and leave track, turning **R** on footpath, scarred by motorbikes, through beechwoods. At obvious crossroads of tracks turn **L**, then bear **R** on forestry track by Shropshire Way sign. Ignore all side turnings until Shropshire Way goes **L** at fork.
❻ Climb gently for while. Where main track levels off and starts to descend, turn **R**. Path leads to Bury Ditches hill fort, then cuts through gap in ramparts and crosses interior. At colour-banded post (red, blue and green), path branches **L** to allow visit to the summit, with its toposcope and incredible views. Bear **R** to return to main path and turn **L** to follow it to car park.

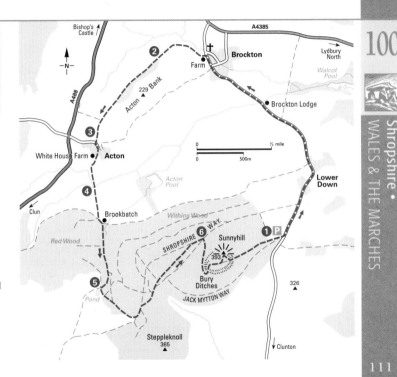

Walking in Safety

All these walks are suitable for any reasonably fit person, but less experienced walkers should try the easier walks first. Route finding is usually straightforward, but you will find that an Ordnance Survey map is a vital addition to the route maps and descriptions.

Risks

Although each walk has been researched with a view to minimising the risks to the walkers who follow its route, no walk in the countryside can be considered to be completely free from risk. Walking in the outdoors will always require a degree of common sense and judgement to ensure that it is as safe as possible.

- Be particularly careful on cliff paths and in upland terrain, where the consequences of a slip can be very serious.

- Remember to check tidal conditions before walking along the seashore.

- Some sections of route are by, or cross roads. Take care and remember traffic is a danger even on minor country lanes.

- Be careful around farmyard machinery and livestock, especially if you have children or a dog with you.

- Be aware of the consequences of changes of weather and check the forecast before you set off. Carry spare clothing and a torch if you are walking in the winter months. Remember that the weather can change very quickly at any time of the year, and in moorland and heathland areas, mist and fog can make route finding much harder. Don't set out in these conditions unless you are confident of your navigation skills in poor visibility. In summer remember to take account of the heat and sun; wear a hat and carry spare water.

- On walks away from centres of population you should carry a whistle and survival bag. If you do have an accident requiring the emergency services, make a note of your position as accurately as possible and dial 999.